THE LANGUAGE LIBRARY

EARLY ENGLISH

THE LANGUAGE LIBRARY

EDITED BY ERIC PARTRIDGE
AND SIMEON POTTER

JOHN WILLIAMS CLARK
UNIVERSITY OF MINNESOTA

EARLY ENGLISH

A STUDY OF
OLD AND MIDDLE ENGLISH

ANDRE DEUTSCH

FIRST PUBLISHED 1957 BY
ANDRE DEUTSCH LIMITED
105 GREAT RUSSELL STREET
LONDON WCI
© JOHN WILLIAMS CLARK 1957, 1967
REVISED EDITION 1967
SECOND IMPRESSION 1970
ALL RIGHTS RESERVED
PRINTED IN GREAT BRITAIN BY
TONBRIDGE PRINTERS LIMITED
TONBRIDGE KENT
ISBN 0 233 95541 0

CONTENTS

IN MEMORIAM
MAGISTRI DILECTISSIMI MEI
MARTIN BRONN RUUD
PH.D., D.C.L., F.R.HIST.S.
1885–1941

PREFACE

The modest objects of this book are set forth in the Introduction; the Reading List, and the occasional footnote references to books and articles not appearing there, will make clear, either implicitly or explicitly, some of the principal sources of information drawn upon; but every student of Early English will realize, as I do all too vividly, how much in the following chapters cannot in practice be specifically credited to this earlier writer or that. That the book does not contain some misstatements and inaccuracies is hardly to be hoped: for such corrections as the learned may offer, I shall try to make a decent pretence of being grateful. I am grateful, quite without pretence, to the publishers, the Messrs Deutsch, for their indulgence of my procrastination; to the learned and gracious Editor of *The Language Library*, Eric Partridge, for innumerable kindnesses; and to my wife, who for her patience under her sufferings during the writing of this book surely deserves a happy issue out of all her afflictions.

JOHN WILLIAMS CLARK

Minneapolis, The Feast of St George, 1957

Chapter I

INTRODUCTION

★

ARISTOTLE and experience agree that man is an inquisitive animal, and most inquisitive, perhaps, about his own relation to the world he inhabits – about his own status and 'how he got that way'. Without going back to ultimates, we may say that he got that way because of his social heritage – because of the behaviour and traditions of his fathers. Occupying the place of indisputable primacy in those traditions are language (the formulation and audible and intelligible communication of human thought and literature in the broad sense, the visibly recorded – or even the more or less perfectly memorized and orally reproduced – perpetuation of that thought). We are almost by natural compulsion, then, interested in how our fathers spoke and wrote and in what they spoke and wrote, and in how differently they spoke and wrote from what and how we speak and write.

Specifically, native speakers of English tend naturally to be curious about how their predecessors in the use of the language 'voiced the reason of their being', and in what those ancients had to say about the subject. How can a lively mind *not* want to know something of such things, if anything can now be known?

And a great deal can be known. We have at our disposal the means of learning much of how our fathers' speech sounded and much more of how they recorded it and of what they thought worth recording. It is the object of this little book to outline and display some of the fundamental parts of this knowledge, without being either a grammar or a history of the language or an anthology or a literary history or an essay in literary criticism; it is designed rather to supply both a prolegomenon and a supplement to all these kinds of books (of which admirable examples already exist and will be found in the reading list) – to present the elements of a number of subjects that the authors of such books sometimes seem (but often only seem, and often

9

with good practical justification) to assume that their readers know about, or can and will find out about elsewhere.

Almost every native speaker of English is inescapably aware that his forefathers spoke and wrote otherwise than he does. He cannot see (or, as people used to say rather more pointedly, hear) *Hamlet* or take part in a Prayer-Book service or read his King James or Douai Bible or hear a new King or Queen proclaimed, without that awareness; and he has very probably, nowadays, had enough schooling to have read a little of the *Canterbury Tales* and to realize that Chaucer's English is in some ways even more different from Cranmer's and Shakespeare's than theirs is from his own. He may even have been given a little taste, at school, of *Beowulf* in the original language, which is so different from his own that he is hard put to it to recognize it as English at all. He is almost certain to know, in short, that there is such a thing as 'Early English'.

Unfortunately, he is very likely to call it – all of it, from *Beowulf* to the Authorized Version – 'old English'. Calling it so would be harmless were it not for the fact that generations of scholars have studied the records of Early English extensively and in detail, that they have been rightly impressed by the differences within Early English no less than by those between it and later English, and that they have long since agreed among themselves to restrict the term 'Old English' (with a capital *O*, note) to a part – the earliest part – of Early English; in other words, 'Old English', technically speaking, is precisely identical with 'Anglo-Saxon'. Chaucer (*c.* 1340–1400) wrote 'old English', if you like, and so did Shakespeare, or Pope, or even Gibbon, but not 'Old English', and though the difference between these two expressions is clear enough in writing, it is not even perceptible in speech. People generally have not altogether taken in this fact of scholarly usage, and as a result they are likely to misunderstand scholars' use of the term 'Old English'.

The term 'Anglo-Saxon' has had a curious history. By the eighth century, the name of southern Britain and that of the language predominantly spoken there (in all its dialects) had come to be commonly 'England' and 'English' respectively, without regard to the fact that the Saxons, at least, were approximately as important as the Angles among the Germanic invaders and settlers of the island. When, therefore, the eighth-century Lombard historian Paulus Diaconus wanted to express the idea 'the Saxons in Britain as distinguished from those still on the Continent', he found *Angli Saxones* a natural and convenient term. Both Paulus and his occasional successors in the use of the expression understood it, however, as meaning 'the *Saxons* of Britain', not 'the Angles, Saxons (and other Germanic inhabitants) of Britain', and still less 'the Angles, Saxons', etc., 'up to the Middle English period': the name of the country universally was 'England', of the people 'Englishmen', and of the language (in all its dialects) 'English', long before that time. The modern use of the term 'Anglo-Saxon' as equivalent to 'Old English' apparently began with the Elizabethan and Jacobean antiquary William Camden, who seems to have taken Paulus Diaconus's *Angli Saxones* – 'insular Saxons' – as *Angli-Saxones* – '(insular) Angles *plus* (insular) Saxons (*et al.*), especially before the Norman Conquest' – and accordingly used 'Anglo-Saxon' as the name of their language. All things considered, 'Old English' is better as the name of the earliest stages of the *language* because it emphasizes the continuous history of that language, but one must admit (1) that that emphasis is perhaps excessive, and (2) that 'Anglo-Saxons' meaning 'the *people* of England up to the Norman Conquest' is sometimes a convenient expression: the Anglo-Saxons did not, indeed, know that they spoke 'Anglo-Saxon', but neither did they know that they spoke '*Old* English'; they felt just as 'English', *tout court*, and just as modern, as we do.

Old English (henceforth usually OE), in the scholars' sense, means English from the time of the earliest extant records (a little before A.D. 700) till *c.* 1100 – *not* till the time of Shakespeare and King James I, or even till the time of Chaucer and *Piers Plowman*. The period from *c.* 1100 till *c.* 1450 is called Middle English (henceforth usually ME), and that from *c.* 1450 till *c.* 1650 is called Early Modern English (henceforth usually ENE – N for 'New'). These dates are all very approximate and more or less arbitrary; depending on the criteria one emphasizes, one may use *c.* 1050 or *c.* 1150 for *c.* 1100, *c.* 1400 or *c.* 1500 for *c.* 1450, and *c.* 1600 or *c.* 1700 for *c.* 1650. The development affected every aspect of language, and was gradual

and for the most part unconscious; people did not stop speaking
OE on 31 December 1099 and begin speaking ME on 1 January
1100, or replace ME with ENE on 25 March 1450. No one can
say on exactly what day childhood becomes youth, or youth
maturity, or maturity old age, but the concepts and the terms
are none the less of great practical use.

In order to gain a real insight into the progress, the causes,
and the manner of these gradual changes, we must not only look
at – and, so far as can be done through reading, 'hear' – specimens
of Early English; we must also take into our minds certain facts
about language families (and even, perhaps, the very concept
of 'language families' itself), about why and how languages
tend to change, about European history and pre-history, about
phonetics (the science or quasi-science dealing with the sounds
of speech), about fashions in handwriting, about paper, pen, and
ink or their analogues, and about the effect of social conditions
on the size and composition of the reading public, on literary
taste, on the kind of literature produced and preserved, and on
the modes and motives of preservation.

First, however, in order not to work in a semi-vacuum, we
had better establish some common ground of conception and
reference. What did Early English, in its several principal stages,
characteristically look like? The method adopted, in the next
chapter, of finding out, though not ideal, is probably the best
practical one.

Chapter II

ENGLISH THROUGH THE CENTURIES: SOME SPECIMENS ANALYSED AND COMPARED

★

BELOW are printed four versions of one of the most familiar passages in the New Testament. In the first column is the Latin of St Jerome's Vulgate,[1] from which all the rest are translated; in the second column an OE (i.e., Anglo-Saxon) version made probably a little before A.D. 1000; in the third, one form of the so-called Wyclif translation (ME) made in the 1380s; and in the fourth, (substantially) Bishop Challoner's revision (1750) of the Reims (-Douai) translation of 1582. (This last is used here instead of the King James or 'Authorized' Version because the latter was translated directly from the original Greek, whereas the NE version here printed depends, like both the earlier English ones, on the Latin and thus makes possible a more exact comparison with them at the same time that it is both modern[2] and designedly very like the Authorized Version.) Since all three translators were doing their best, according to their lights and the linguistic standards of their times, to reproduce, exactly, the sense of the same source, and since all three use

---

[1] 'Vulgate' means 'translated into the vulgar, i.e., the common tongue.' Literally, it could denominate any translation from the original biblical languages, Hebrew and Greek (and Aramaic), into the vernacular of a people unaccustomed to at least the colloquial use of those languages; historically speaking, '*the* Vulgate' means the translation into Latin – then and in western Europe the 'vulgar' tongue – made by St Jerome toward the end of the fourth century A.D. Though often itself subsequently translated, and though now in the process of being (very slowly) succeeded by a new official Latin translation, it was for a very long time, in the main still is, and will always in a sense remain *the* Bible of western Europe.

[2] Relatively modern, that is; neither the Reims-Douai, even 'modernized,' nor the King James version, of course, is in quite the language of the twentieth century, except (in modern reprints) in spelling.

what may be called the normal English of their times, we could
hardly find a more dependable basis for a fair and objective
comparison of the stages of the English language at the three
periods represented. (The Latin text given here, incidentally,

[1] Factum est autem in diebus
illis, exiit edictum a Caesare
Augusto ut describeretur universus
orbis.

Soþlice on þam dagum wæs
geworden gebod fram þam Casere
Augusto þæt eall ymbehwyrft wære
tomearcod.

[2] Haec descriptio prima facta est
a praeside Syriae Cyrino:

þeos tomearcodnes wæs ærest
geworden fram þam deman Syrige,
Cirino.

[3] Et ibant omnes ut profiteren-
tur singuli in suam civitatem.

And ealle hig eodon . . . and syndrie
ferdon on hyra ceastre.

[4] Ascendit autem et Joseph a
Galilaea de civitate Nazareth in
Judaeam in civitatem David, quae
vocatur Bethlehem: eo quod esset
de domo et familia David,

þa ferde Iosep from Galilea, of
þære ceastre Nazareth, on Iudeisce,
ceastre Dauides, seo is genemned
Bethleem, forþam he wæs of
Dauides huse and hirede,

[5] Ut profiteretur cum Maria
desponsata sibi uxore praegnante.

þæt he ferde[1] mid Marian, þe him
beweddod wæs and wæs ge-eacnod.

[6] Factum est autem, cum essent
ibi, impleti sunt dies ut pareret.

Soþlice wæs geworden, þa hi þar
wæron, hire dagas wæron gefyllede
þæt heo cende.

[7] Et peperit filium suum primo-
genitum, et pannis eum involvit, et
reclinavit eum in praesepio: quia
non erat eis locus in diversorio.

And heo cende hyre frumcennedan
sunu, ond hine mid cildclaþum
bewand, and hine on binne alede,
forþam þe hig næfdon rum on
cumena huse.

[8] Et pastores erant in regione
eadem vigilantes, et custodientes
vigilias noctis super gregem suum.

And hyrdas wæron on þam ylcan
rice, waciende and niht-wæccan
healdende ofer heora heorda.

[9] Et ecce angelus Domini stetit
juxta illos, et claritas Dei circumful-
sit illos, et timuerunt timore magno.

þa stod Drihtnes engel wiþ hig, and
Godes beorhtnes him ymbescean;
and hi him mycelum ege adredon.

[10] Et dixit illis angelus: Nolite
timere: ecce enim evangelizo vobis
gaudium magnum, quod erit omni
populo:

And se engel him to cwæþ, Nelle
ge eow adrædan; soþlice nu! Ic eow
bodie mycelne gefean, se biþ eallum
folce.

[1] A mistranslation; neither here nor in verse 3, above, has the OE
translator understood *profitere(n)tur*. He probably confused it with
proficiscere(n)tur.

is a 'classicized' and normalized one; both OE and ME translators would have known a Latin text in which *æ* was normally represented by *e*, *v* by *u* (except initially, where *u* would contrarily be represented by *v*), *j* by *i*, *-tio* often by *-cio*, etc.)

Forsothe it was don in tho dayes, a maundement went out fro Cesar August that al the world schulde be discryued.	And it came to pass that in those days there went out a decree from Caesar Augustus that the whole world should be enrolled.
This firste discryuyng was maad of Cyryne, iustice of Cirye.	This enrolling was first made by Cyrinus, the governor of Syria.
And alle men wenten, that thei schulde make professioun, ech by him self in to his cite.	And all went to be enrolled, every one into his own city.
Sothly and Josep stiȝede vp fro Galilee, of the cite of Nazareth, in to Jude, in to a cite of Dauith, that is clepid Bedleem, for that he was of the hous and meyne of Dauith,	And Joseph also went up from Galilee, out of the city of Nazareth, into Judea, to the city of David, which is called Bethlehem: because he was of the house and family of David,
That he schulde knowleche with Marie, with child spousid wyf to him.	To be enrolled with Mary his espoused wife, who was with child.
Sothli it was don, whanne thei weren there, the dayes weren fulfillid that she schulde bere child.	And it came to pass that when they were there, her days were accomplished that she should be delivered.
And sche childide her firste born sone, and wlappide him in clothis, and puttide him in a cracche, for ther was not place to hym in the comyn stable.	And she brought forth her firstborn son and wrapped him up in swaddling clothes and laid him in a manger: because there was no room for them in the inn.
And schepherdis weren in the same contre, wakinge and kepinge the watchis of the nyȝt on her flok.	And there were in the same country shepherds watching and keeping the night watches over their flock.
And loo! the aungel of the Lord stood by sydis hem, and the clerenesse of God schynede aboute hem; and thei dredden with greet drede.	And behold an angel of the Lord stood by them and the brightness of God shone round about them: and they feared with a great fear.
And the aungel seide to hem, Nyle ȝe drede; lo! sothli I euangelise to ȝou a grete ioye, that schal be to al peple.	And the angel said to them: Fear not; for behold, I bring you good tidings of great joy that shall be to all the people:

[11] Quia natus est vobis hodie Salvator, qui est Christus Dominus, in civitate David.

Forþam todæg eow ys hælend acenned, se is Drihten Crist, on Dauides ceastre.

[12] Et hoc vobis signum: Invenietis infantem pannis involutum, et positum in praesepio.

And þis tacen eow byþ; ge gemetaþ an cild hræglum bewunden, and on binne aled.

[13] Et subito facta est cum angelo multitudo militiae coelestis laudantium Deum, et dicentium:

And þa wæs færinga geworden mid þam engle mycelnes heofonlices werydes, God herigendra, and þus cweþendra.

[14] Gloria in altissimis[1] Deo, et in terra pax hominibus bonae voluntatis.

Gode sy wuldor on heahnesse, and on eorþan sybb mannum godes willan.

---

[1] Though it perhaps does not exactly concern the English language, it does concern English and European culture to observe (1) that the wording of the Mass, 'Gloria in *excelsis* Deo', is older than the Vulgate (which is over 1,500 years old!) – i.e., goes back to a time before there was any official Latin translation of the Greek New Testament as a whole; and (2) that the Prayer-Book *Gloria*, with its 'Glory be to God *on high*', reflects the *excelsis* of the Latin Mass (as does the OE version in column 2) whereas the Authorized Version's 'Glory be to God *in the highest*' reflects the Vulgate's *altissimis*. The original Greek is ὑψίστοις (hupsistois), which is more literally rendered by '*altissimis*' and 'the highest'; but, in both Latin and English, the freer and what we may call the popular renderings of the word characteristically retained their places in the Eucharist, which was, until at least the latter part of the sixteenth century, more familiar to most people than the biblical text itself. What the people knew in both ages and languages, i.e., was not the scholars' rendering, but the parish priests' rendering. An even more striking example of the same thing is to be found in the universal English version – both before and after the Reformation, both Catholic and Protestant – of the *Gloria Patri*, where 'and to the Holy Ghost; as it was in the beginning, is now, and ever shall be' ought to be 'and to the Holy Ghost; as it was in the beginning, so be it now and ever.'

For a sauyour is borun to day to vs, that is Crist the Lord, in the cite of Dauith.	For this day is born to you a Saviour, who is Christ the Lord, in the city of David.
And this a tokene to ȝou; ȝe sculen fynde a ȝong child wlappid in clothis, and put in a cracche.	And this shall be a sign unto you. You shall find the infant wrapped in swaddling clothes and laid in a manger.
And sudenly ther is maad with the aungel a multitude of heuenly knyȝthod, heriynge God, and seyinge,	And suddenly there was with the angel a multitude of the heavenly army, praising God and saying:
Glorie in the hiȝeste thingis to God, and in erthe pees to men of good wille.	Glory to God in the highest: and on earth peace to men of good will.

A mere first glance at the three translations will show (1) that they are very different, and (2) that the second (ME) is much more like the third (NE) than it is like the first (OE); a very little further inspection of the three translations will show (1) that the first (OE) is practically unintelligible, or at the very least would be to a reader unacquainted with some other version, and (2) that the second (ME) is fundamentally even more easily intelligible (i.e., in effect, in most ways even more like the NE) than it seems at first sight. We have already learnt at least two very important facts: (1) that English changed very greatly over 750 years, and (2) that it changed much more rapidly and radically during the first half of that period than during the second.[1]

The reasons for this latter fact are important and interesting, but before we deal with them let us re-examine the three English translations, this time in a more closely observant and analytical way. We shall discover that the differences (i.e., those observable from reading the foregoing printed texts) between the first and the second English translations, and to a lesser degree between the second and the third, can be classified as differences in (1) spelling, (2) strange letters and uses of letters, (3) vocabulary, (4) idiom, (5) inflexion, (6) number of words (i.e., length of passage), and (7) order of words.

Spelling is put first because it is probably the most conspicuous, deceptive, and bothersome (though yet, in a way, the

[1] Except for one feature, pronunciation, but this is only obscurely reflected in the written form, and must be left for later treatment.

least fundamental). Both the second (OE) and the third (ME) columns contain many words that are still in common use, but whose familiarity is veiled by spellings not only different from those we are used to but also inconsistent. Thus, in verse 1 of the second column, *soþ-* is now *sooth*, *wæs* is *was*, *þæt* is *that*, *eall* is *all*, *-mearcod* is *marked*, and *wære* is *were;* and in the same verse of the third column (ME), *-sothe* is now *sooth*, *don* is *done*, *dayes* is *days*, *maundement* is *(com)mandment*, and *schulde* is *should*. As for inconsistency, cf., in the second column (OE), *hig* (verse 3) and *hi* (v. 6); and, in the third column (ME), *she* (v. 6) and *sche* (v. 7). Our habit nowadays is almost always to spell the same *word* in the same way, though we often spell the same *sound* in *different* ways. Our predecessors, on the other hand, commonly used, with little system, any of several *spellings* for the same *sound*, even in several successive instances of the same *word* in the same ms. C. A.D. 1000, *hig* and *hi* were equally acceptable spellings of the sound heard today in *he*, and *c*. 1380 *she* and *sche* were equally acceptable spellings of (approximately) the sound heard today in *shay;* and any writer might and often did spell inconsistently.[1]

Next come strange letters and uses of letters. Column 2 (OE) has *þ* for *th* and only by accident lacks examples of another letter, *ð*, with the same value; it also has *æ* (formally *a* plus *e*, but regarded during the period of its use as more or less a distinct and single letter and pronounced like the *a* in *hat* – *a* by itself having represented the *a* of *father*). Column 3 (ME) has *ȝ*, with two values, one as in *nyȝt* (v. 8), where it represents what is represented in modern German by the *ch* of *nicht* or *Nacht* (approximately the same as *ch* in Scottish *loch*), and the other as in *ȝong* (v. 12), where it represents the consonant sound of NE *y*. Column 3 (ME) also occasionally uses *i* for *j* (as in *iustice*, v. 2), *v* for *u* (as in *vp*, v. 4), and *u* for *v* (as in *euangelise*, v. 10); and it uses *i* and *y* almost interchangeably.

The differences in vocabulary are, at least after the first glance, the most impressive of all, and in some ways the most important. Most impressive and most important, i.e., as between OE on the

---

[1] Though almost always within certain limits – *she* appears in the fourteenth century as *she, sche, shee, schee, sse,* and *ssee* (etc.!), but never, e.g., as 'sze' or 'shay'.

one hand and ME and NE together on the other. Apart from proper names, the OE passage uses ninety-four distinct words (discounting inflexional forms of the same words, but including as separate words most of the several elements of compounds). Of these, twenty-one are wholly obsolete: (verse 1) *ymbe*, preposition and adverb (here a prefix), 'around'; *hwyrft*, noun (here part of a compound), 'wheel, circle'; *gebod*, noun, 'commandment, decree'; (v. 2) *deman*, noun, 'judge, governor'; (v. 3) *eodon*, verb, 'went'; (v. 4) *genemned*, past participle, 'named'; *hirede*, noun, 'family'; (v. 5) *þe*, relative pronoun, 'who'; *ge-eacnod*, past participle, 'enlarged' (i.e., 'pregnant'); (v. 6) *cende*, verb, 'bore'; *þa*, adverb, 'when'; (v. 7) *frum*, adverb (here a prefix), 'first'; *cumena*, noun, '(of) travellers'; (v. 9) *Drihtnes*, noun, '(of the) Lord'; *engel*, noun, 'angel'; *ege*, noun, 'awe'; (v. 10) *gefean*, noun, 'joy'; (v. 13) *færinga*, adverb, 'suddenly'; *werod*, noun, 'army, host'; *herigendra*, present participle, 'praising'; (v. 14) *wuldor*, noun, 'glory'. Of these twenty-one words, nine are more or less closely related to words still in use: *hwyrft* to *whirl*, *gebod* to (*for*)*bode*, *deman* to *deem* and *doom*, *nemnan* to *name*, *ge-eacnod* to *eke*, *cende* to *kin*, *frum* to *former*, *cumena* to *come*, and (in a somewhat different way) *engel* to *angel*.

Another fourteen may be just barely said to retain a sort of place in the language: (verse 1) *soþlice*, adverb, 'truly' – we still have a noun *sooth* and an adverbial termination -*ly*; *geworden*, past participle, 'become' – the third-person present singular indicative of the verb survives in the proverbial catch-phrase 'Woe worth the day' (where 'worth' means 'become', or rather 'come (to)', 'day' here having been originally dative); (v. 2) *tomearcodnes*, noun, '(a) marking apart', translating *descriptio* (too literally) – survives only formally, and only without the prefix *to-*, and only if 'markedness' can be called a word; (v. 3) *hig*, pronoun, 'they' – other forms of the same pronoun survive in *he*, *him*, *his*, *her*, and *it* (earlier *hit*); *ceastre*, noun, 'city' – survives in such place-names as *Chester*, *Manchester*, *Doncaster*, *Gloucester*, and *Exeter* (and *Caister* and *Castor*); (v. 5) *mid*, preposition, 'with' – survives only as the prefix of *midwife*; (v. 7) *n*(*æfdon*), 'had not', compound of *n*(*e*), 'not', with (*h*)*æfdon*, 'had' – the negative particle attached in this way to a verb survives only in *willy-nilly;* (v. 8) *hyrdas,* noun, 'herds-men' – survives in the second element of *shepherds,* etc.; *ylcan,* adjective, 'same' – survives, in correct use, only in *MacGregor* (etc.) *of that ilk; rice,* noun, 'kingdom, country, district' – survives in *bishopric;* (v. 9) *wiþ,* preposition, '(over) against' – survives formally in NE *with,* but semantically only in words like *withstand; mycelum,* adjective, 'much, great' – survives, in ordinary English, only in 'Many a mickle makes a muckle'; (v. 10) *cwæþ,* verb, 'said' – survives only in the archaic *quoth(a);* *hræglum,* noun, 'clothes' – survives only in *nightrail.*

In order to count as many as fifty-nine words as remaining in full use in NE we must be very generous. Eight compound verbs can be said to be still in use only if we disregard the prefixes and count only the verbs proper – and some of them are not used in the same senses: (verse 1) *tomearcod,* past participle, 'marked apart', (too literally) translating (with *wære,* 'should be') *describeretur;* (v. 5) *beweddod,* past participle, 'wedded'; (v. 6) *gefyllede,* past participle, '(ful)filled'; (v. 7) *bewand,* 'wound' (which, however, we hardly use for 'wrapped'); (v. 9) (*ymbe*)*scean,* 'shone (round about)'; *adredon,* 'dreaded'; (v. 12) *aled,* 'laid'; *gemetaþ,* 'meet with, come upon, find'. Finally, there are six other words that can be regarded as still in use only by stretching a point of a different kind: (verse 3) *ferdon* survives formally as 'ferried', but the sense and the construction are somewhat different; (v. 4) *seo* and (v. 11) *se* are the nominative singular feminine and masculine, respectively, of a demonstrative pronoun whose other forms all begin with *th,* and several of these forms are reflected in *the, that,* and *tho(se);* (v. 7) *binne* is 'bin', which, however, we hardly substitute for 'manger'; (v. 10) *bodie* remains in 'It bodes ill', but 'bodes' in that expression means 'foreshadows' rather than 'announces'; (v. 11) *Hælend* is the present participle of 'heal', but instead of calling Christ '(the) Healing (One), (the One) making healthy', we use 'Saviour', derived from *Salvator(em),* the word translated (literally and perhaps not very felicitously) by *Hælend;* (v. 14) *sibb* is 'sib', which now means, however, 'kindred' and sometimes other things, but not 'peace'.

The remaining forty-five words – a little less than half the whole number of distinct words in the OE version – are still in use in at least nearly the same forms and in virtually or exactly the same senses.

When we come to the vocabulary of the ME version (column 3) the situation is very different; not more than a dozen words there have disappeared from the language, and the meaning even of several of these is transparent, at least in context. *Maundement* (verse 1) is '(com)mandment', *discryued* (roughly speaking) is formally NE 'described' but means here 'enrolled (in a tax list)', *stiȝede* (v. 4) means 'went up', *clepid* means 'called' (past participle), *meyne*, though now rare, is still listed in most dictionaries (under *meinie* or *meiny*) as 'retinue' (here it means rather 'family'), *knowleche* (v. 5) is formally '(ac)knowledge' but means here something like 'testify formally to his tax status', *childide* pretty obviously means 'bore a child', *wlappide* means 'wrapped', *cracche* is modern French *crèche* ('manger'), *her* (v. 8) and *hem* (v. 9) mean 'their' and 'them' respectively, and *nyle* is *n(e)* ('not') plus *(w)yle* ('be willing') – i.e., 'don't be willing'. Of these eleven words (counting *her* and *hem* as one, as we may properly do), seven are native English words, and are (most of them) absent from the OE version only by accident, but the remaining four (*maundement*, *discryued*, *meyne*, and *cracche*) are French loan-words,[1] and *their* absence from the OE version is not accidental at all, for English borrowed almost no French words till about a century after the OE translation was made. But *c.* A.D. 1100, it began borrowing them in increasing numbers, along with others directly from Latin – a great many more than it had borrowed from that source (or from any) before the Norman Conquest.

The ME version uses one hundred and one words, not counting proper names or more than one inflexional form of any word (note that this figure is not significantly greater than the ninety-four of the OE version). Of these hundred and one, twenty-five are loan-words, distributed according to source as follows: Nineteen are certainly and three others probably taken from French, these three being *profescioun* (verse 3), *euangelise* (v. 10), and *multitude* (v. 13), which may have come directly from Latin instead of indirectly, through French, as all the nineteen do except one. That one is *cracche*, which, though immediately from

[1] Loan-words – words borrowed from other languages.

French, is ultimately from Frankish, a Germanic language, closely related to English, anciently spoken in the north of what is now France (which, indeed, derives its name from the Franks, who also, it is evident, contributed a good many words to the otherwise Latin speech of Romanized Gaul). Of the twenty-two words certainly or possibly from French, two – *euangelise*, and *aungel* (v. 9) – are ultimately Greek. Four of the French words are combined with native English suffixes – *discryu(ed)* (v. 1), *spous(id)* (v. 5), *clere(nesse)* (v. 9), and *suden(ly)* (v. 13). The remaining three of the twenty-five loan-words come from Old Norse (henceforth usually ON), another ancient Germanic language closely allied to English – *fro* (v. 1), *thei* (v. 3), and *same* (v. 8).

Clearly, between *c.* 1000 and *c.* 1380, English had (1) borrowed a great many French words and a smaller number of ON ones, (2) naturalized at least some of these words to such an extent as to attach native suffixes to them freely, and (3) lost a good many native words (though hardly quite so many as this passage seems to suggest). The only loan-words in the OE version are *ceastre* (v. 3), from Latin *castrum*, and *engel* (v. 9), from Latin *angelus* (ultimately Greek, like a good many words from Latin either directly or through French).[1]

The NE version (column 4) has thirty-nine words not in the ME version (column 3), but all thirty-nine occurred in ME, and are absent here only more or less accidentally.[2] Of the thirty-nine, nineteen are pure native words used as they were in OE (and ME); three more are pure native words, but used otherwise

---

[1] OE *engel* disappeared but was replaced in ME in the course of time by *a(u)ngel*, from French, which got it from Latin, which got it in turn from the same Greek word as had ultimately supplied OE *engel*. NE *angel* is from ME *a(u)ngel*, not from OE *engel*, which would probably have yielded NE **ingle*. (The actual NE word *ingle* has nothing to do with it.) Note, in connexion with **ingle*, that an asterisk *before* a word means that the form is hypothetical – i.e., that it probably, not certainly, existed or would exist, given normal conditions.

[2] Five of these, incidentally, though missing from the ME version, occur in both the OE and the NE: (verse 9) *beorhtnes-brightness* (ME *clerenesse*), (v. 1) *fram-from* (ME *fro*), (v. 7) *(a)lede-laid* (ME *puttide*), (v. 8) *ofer-over* (ME *on*.), (v. 7) *rum-room* (ME *place*). But this also is largely accidental.

than they were in OE – *which* (v. 4) and *who* (v. 11), which were not used as relative pronouns till ME, and *you*, which is never nominative (only dative and accusative) in OE and seldom in ME. Two others, *swaddling* (v. 7) and *unto* (v. 12), do not occur till ME, but are made up of OE elements; and finally, one word, *wrapped*, is not recorded till ME, but is probably native, and certainly not French. The remaining fourteen words are French (and ultimately Latin). (Strictly speaking, one of them is only mainly French – *because* (v. 4) is native *by* plus French *cause*.)

Some of these figures probably give the impression that the fundamental part of the vocabulary changed somewhat more between OE and ME, and much more between ME and NE, than it actually did. It is indeed true that many of the differences between the vocabularies of the three versions (especially of two immediately consecutive ones) are more or less accidental, and might well have been somewhat fewer if the translations had been made by other writers; particularly, of the many words that are found in the OE version but not in the ME or the NE, and that are obsolete or virtually so today, a good many more than half were still more or less current in at least some ME dialects. But it is none the less significant that it did not occur to the ME translator to use them; and besides, the possibly exaggerated impression of changes in what we may call the potential vocabulary of daily life as a whole is pretty well counterbalanced by the fact that if the text were, say, a treatise on astronomy or political theory rather than a simple and homely narrative (and such treatises were produced, particularly in the ME period), the differences in vocabulary, especially in the number of (mostly Latin and French) loan-words, would be greater, not less. In short, the several versions of the passage show rather more change than actually occurred in the total potential vocabulary of daily life, but rather less than occurred in the vocabulary of the language as a whole.

As soon as we pass from single words considered in isolation to phrases, combinations, and constructions, we discover yet another important difference among all three versions, a difference in idiom. Taking first OE and then ME, let us translate some of the conspicuous examples literally into NE, and observe how unnatural they seem – and yet they were perfectly natural in their own day.

OE. (verse 1) *on þam dagum* – 'on those days'; *eall ymbehwyrft,* 'all [*the*] world'; *wære tomearcod,* 'were [instead of "should be"] registered'; (v. 7) *hig næfdon rum on cumena huse,* 'they *not-had* room *on* [*the*] travellers' house'; (v. 14) *Gode sy wuldor on heahnesse,* '[*to*] God be glory *on* [*the*] highness'.

ME. (v. 2) 'was maad *of* Cyryne'; (v. 4) 'for *that* he was'; (v. 6) 'she schulde bere [*her*] child'; (v. 7) 'ther was not [*a*] place *to* [them]'; (v. 9) 'by syd*is* [them]'.

Next, differences in inflexion. Inflexion is the modification of words – most commonly of the endings of words – according to the function of the words in a sentence. NE uses very few inflexions; the most conspicuous and frequent are the final -(*e*)*s,* -*'s,* and -(*e*)*s'* of the possessives and plurals of most nouns (*hen, hens, hen's, hens'; ass, asses, ass's, asses'*), the final -(*e*)*s* of the third-person singular present of most verbs (*I sing, he sings; I reach, he reaches*), the -*ed* of the past tense and past participle of most verbs (*look, looked*), the changing vowel in the correspond-ing forms of a smaller number of verbs (*sing, sang, sung*), the -*er* and -*est* of the comparative and superlative degrees of most adjectives (*small, smaller, smallest*), and the different forms for different cases, genders, and numbers of some pronouns (third-person nominative singular masculine *he,* feminine *she,* neuter *it;* objective *him, her, it;* possesive *his, her, its;* plural *they, them, their;* etc.). NE has a few other inflexions, but they are com-paratively rare. It has, indeed, fewer inflexions than all but one or two of the languages related to it. In times past it had many more, as we shall see by looking again at the OE passage above, and, somewhat less clearly, at the ME one as well.

In verse 1 of the OE version, *þam dagum* has the form peculiar to the dative (and instrumental) plural; the equivalent phrases in the ME and NE versions – *tho dayes* and *those days* – are inflected as plural, but not as of any particular case. Again, in v. 3, *eodon* is marked as (third-person) preterite[1] plural indicative (the singular would be *eode*), and likewise, in v. 3 of the ME the corresponding *wenten* is distinguished as plural from the singular, which would be *wente,* whereas the NE has *went* without inflexion

[1] *Preterite* – an occasionally convenient substitute for *past*(-)*tense.*

for number. And inflexion affects not only the forms of words, but also their number. Thus v. 4 of the OE has *ceastre Dauides* (the *-es* showing that the word is here in the genitive case and means 'David's' or 'of David'). For this the ME and NE substitute 'a cite of Dauith' and 'the city of David'. The genitive case form 'Dauithes' existed in ME, and 'David's' exists in NE, but, in both, the tendency with such expressions is to use *of*-phrases rather than the genitive case with its distinctive ending – and, concomitantly, to use four words rather than two. Note also that in NE (and ME), if one were to write 'David's' instead of 'of David', one would invariably put it before 'city', whereas in OE it may equally well (and here does) come after.

Many more of the words in the OE version appear with their endings more or less distinctively inflected for case, number, and gender (nouns, pronouns, and adjectives) or for person, number, mood, and tense (verbs) – much more variously than in NE. The ME version is inflected much less elaborately than the OE, but essentially not so much less so as appears on the surface. In verse 5, e.g., the final *e* of *schulde* is not merely an unpronounced letter that may or may not conclude a word (as it might be in 'should(e)' in, say, the Shakespeare First Folio of 1623, which is in ENE), but an essential part of the form usual *c.* 1380, and pronounced as a syllable.

Next, if we count the words in the three passages (including, this time, proper names, and each word each time it occurs) we find that the OE version is about 220 words long, the ME about 275, and the NE about 285 (absolute precision is made almost impossible by the difficulty of deciding which compounds to count as one word and which as two or more). The difference here between the ME and the NE is practically inconsiderable; but that between them and the OE is characteristic and significant. We have already seen that the reduction in the number of inflected forms between OE and ME leads, sometimes, to a multiplication of words, by the substitution of phrases for single words (e.g., 'of Dauith' for 'Dauides'); and the words are still further multiplied, in ME and yet more in NE, by the more frequent use of *a*(*n*) and *the*.

A final difference shown by the OE from the ME and NE is in freedom of word order. One might say in OE almost indifferently

either *hine on binne alede* (verse 7) and *se engel him to cwæp*
(v. 10) or 'alede hine on binne' and 'se engel cwæþ to him'; but
it would be quite unnatural, at least in ordinary prose, to say
'him in a cracche puttide' and 'the aungel hem to seide' in (at
least this kind of) ME, or 'him in a manger laid' or 'the angel
them to said' in NE. Word order in OE, i.e., is relatively free;
in ME and NE, relatively fixed. This difference, like the difference
in number of words, is partly owing to the falling together of
similar sounds and to the consequent reduction in the number
of distinctive inflexions: when the functions and relations of
words cease to be shown clearly or at all by modifications of
form, the tendency is to show them by a relatively unvarying
position. It is true that there seems to be some reason for thinking that it was the other way round – that the adoption of a
relatively unvarying word order preceded and made practical
the reduction in the number of distinctive inflexions, instead of
following and being caused by it. The resolution of this conflict
(so far as it is not a matter of which came first, the chicken or
the egg) is probably to be found in the fact that writing never
quite catches up with speech, and that we are naturally too prone
to forget that fact and to assume that writing reflects contemporary speech more exactly than it does. Scribal convention
and tradition long preserved – though very imperfectly – certain
orthographical distinctions that no longer reflected actual speech,
with the result that the written records of English of, say, 1050
suggest a more archaic pronunciation – and the preservation of
a greater number of distinctive *spoken* forms – than actually
obtained in contemporary speech. We still do much the same
sort of thing: *bow*, in NE, may sound like *bough* or *beau*, depending
on the sense. If Late Old English (henceforth LOE) scribes had
been *completely and consistently* conservative in their spelling, we
should know much less than we do about the change in both
pronunciation and about which came first – that change, or the
change in word order; but in practice the scribes often forgot
their own 'rules' and tell us things that they didn't mean to tell
us. In short, the documents *prima facie* suggest that the word
order changed before the pronunciation; further examination
and reflection suggest, on the whole, rather the opposite.

At this point it would seem reasonable to go on, from such

kinds of differences between Early English and NE as we have discussed, to two others – differences in pronunciation and differences in handwriting. It is more practical, however, to deal first with two other subjects: when and how English came to Britain, and how it is related to certain other languages.

Chapter III

THE COUSINS OF ENGLISH

THE INDO-EUROPEAN, ESPECIALLY THE GERMANIC, LANGUAGES

★

IT IS easy to forget that England has not always been 'England'. From the dawn of history till *c.* A.D. 450 it was Britain. There was, indeed, an 'England' for centuries before 450, but it was on the Continent, not in Britain, and it was probably not always the same place, but was rather whatever district was inhabited for the time being by the Germanic tribes that sooner or later came to call themselves by various early forms of the name English or Angles. Our Germanic ancestors had the habit, convenient and natural for them however confusing for their descendants, of giving their name to whatever country they were inhabiting at the time, just as today John Smith, if he removes his family from 'a dismal and illiberal life in Camberwell' to 'a dismal and illiberal life in Islington', still calls his house 'John Smith's house'. All names, however, must have a beginning, and the English, or Angles, presumably took their name from a district in Schleswig still called Angel[1] (apparently meaning 'the corner', 'the angular region'). (Where they may have dwelt before, and what they may have called themselves, no one can say.) But just as the present meaning of 'England' does not indicate that the English originated there, so the present meaning of the Danish 'Angel' does not indicate that the English were necessarily living there just before they came to Britain. Every English child has been brought up on the tradition, going back to the Venerable Bede (673–735), that Britain was invaded and settled from *c.* 450 onwards by three Germanic tribes, Angles, Saxons, and Jutes. But (1) there is good reason to

---

[1] Pronounced [ˈaŋgl̩], not [ˈeindʒl̩] (for these phonetic symbols, see the next chapter), and quite unrelated to NE *angel*; the identity of the spelling is an historical accident.

believe that he should have mentioned Frisians as well, and even, perhaps, other Germanic tribes, and (2) there is little reason to feel sure that, when they invaded Britain, the Angles, the Saxons, and the Jutes came precisely or exclusively or even at all from what were earlier or later known as Angel, Jutland, or Saxony (and very certainly the Saxons did not come from what is *now* called Saxony). All we can say with much assurance is this: Britain was invaded and largely settled, over about a century from *c.* 450, by successive parties and troops of Germanic tribesmen living at the time along or near the coast of the North Sea from what is now (nearly or quite northern) Denmark, nearly or quite to what is now northern Belgium; these tribes spoke dialects mutually intelligible and probably regarded (rightly) by their speakers as mere regional varieties of a single language; groups whose dominant members, at least, called themselves English or Angles occupied the central and largest part of (southern) Britain; and in the course of time their names for themselves and their new country – as Latinized, *Angli*, *Anglia* – became more or less accidentally applied to at least the whole southern part of the island of Great Britain and to at least its Germanic inhabitants. King Alfred ($\overset{c}{\wedge}$849–$\overset{c}{\wedge}$899) was a (West) Saxon, and ruled the kingdom of Wessex (i.e., of the West Saxons), but he calls his language English, not Saxon or Anglo-Saxon: indeed, the extension of the name of the language seems to have been earlier than that of the people and the country, so that in a sense the concept or at least the name of 'the English language' is older than that of 'the English people' or 'England'.

English has been spoken of above as a member of 'the Germanic family of languages'. Before we proceed further with English, let us see what is meant by 'family of languages'.

The general idea is not hard to grasp. In the first place, the reason why a language family is so called is that in some important ways it closely resembles a family of people. The languages of a language family, that is, have a common ancestor, very much as the members of a human family have. In the second place, we are all familiar with small families of closely related languages – e.g., the English of London, the English of Manchester, the English of Edinburgh, the English of Dublin, and the English of New York. We are not in the habit, indeed, of giving to these several kinds of English the name 'languages', or, it may be, even 'dialects'; we usually in practice reserve these names, or at least the first of them, for modes of speech more fundamentally and conspicuously different from each other than the English of London, the English of Manchester, etc. But the distinction between 'language' and 'dialect', or between 'dialect' and 'local variety', however useful, is not essential or philosophical: the several kinds of English mentioned above do constitute a family of 'languages' in that they are different but have a common ancestor – are, in other words, divergent developments of a single earlier form of speech.

An example only a little less familiar and perhaps, by compensation, more readily acceptable and convincing, is what are called the Romance languages. No one who has studied even a little French and Italian can escape the realization that the two languages are fundamentally and closely *related* – by which we mean that they have a (not very remote) common ancestor – by which we mean, in turn, that some single earlier language developed differently in different places: in Italy, into Italian, and in France, into French. The 'single earlier language' was, of course, Latin – the everyday, familiar spoken Latin of the lower classes in various parts of the Roman Empire from one or two centuries B.C. to one or two A.D. Besides (standard) French and (standard) Italian, the Romance languages include (Castilian or standard) Spanish, Catalan (spoken in north-eastern Spain), Galician (spoken in north-western Spain), Portuguese, Provençal (spoken in southern France), Rumanian, and several others less well known. They are called 'Romance', pretty obviously, because they are spoken by people whose ancestors – or rather whose cultural predecessors – regarded themselves as Romans, i.e., as citizens of the Roman Empire, and spoke, or at least understood, a variety of the 'Roman' language. (The name 'Latin' tended to be rather arbitrarily reserved, as it still does, for the relatively polished, conservative, and stable language of learning and public affairs. It is somewhat as if the language of the present Archbishop of Canterbury were to be called 'English' and the language of his boot-black 'British', or vice versa.)

Nothing can be more obvious or more certain than that French, Italian, Spanish, etc., are members of a single family of languages. It is equally certain, though not equally well known to so many people from their own observation, and far from equally obvious on the surface, that Latin, the ancestor of French and Italian, is itself a member of the same family as English – and for that matter, of the same family as Greek, Russian, and Hindi. (In some superficial ways, Latin seems more closely related to English than it is, because of the large number of Latin words borrowed by ME and NE. It seems much *less* closely related, on the other hand, to OE, which had borrowed comparatively few words from it; and yet it *is* related to OE, and would be so even if it had 'lent' OE no words at all.)

The great language family to which English (Old, Middle, and Modern alike), Latin, Russian, etc., all belong has been called by various names – Japhetic, Aryan, Indo-Germanic, Indo-European – none of which is in every way satisfactory, but the last of which, Indo-European, though the clumsiest, is perhaps now the commonest. Note that this term (henceforth usually IE) is used in two somewhat different ways: (1) as the name of the family (the IE *languages*), and (2) as the name of the family's prehistoric common ancestor (the IE *language*).

IE (in the second sense) was spoken probably at least as late as about 3000 B.C. by a people or group of peoples living in a territory of uncertain extent of which the centre was most probably not far from Poland.[1] So far as is known, IE is unrelated to any other language (with the single exception of Hittite, spoken in Asia Minor about 1500 B.C.), though some students think it may eventually prove to be very remotely related to one or more groups of languages spoken in historical times by neighbouring peoples.

The speakers of IE may well have been racially hybrid and

[1] The words 'probably', 'about', and 'uncertain' in this sentence are necessary qualifications; it is easy to forget how little we know directly about most of the ancestors of most Europeans and many Asians until shortly before the Christian era, though we know quite a lot about such of their more civilized contemporaries of other stocks – and speaking other languages – as the Egyptians, the Babylonians, the Assyrians, the Hebrews, and the Chinese.

politically disunited, but in language and, largely, culture they were certainly at one time a single people. From time to time, tribes or groups of tribes wandered away from the homeland in various directions and to various distances, and lost both mutual contact and the memory of their earlier connexion. In their respective new homes, they usually met and often intermarried with peoples speaking languages of various other families. These meetings, and concomitant circumstances, had a number of effects: the speakers of IE often borrowed some words from the languages of their new neighbours and always dropped some of their own; others of their own they used in progressively divergent senses; their new neighbours sometimes took to speaking IE, into which they imported sounds, words, idioms, and constructions from their own non-IE languages – sounds, words, etc., that were sometimes adopted by the native speakers of IE, especially when they became outnumbered by their new neighbours. This process of differentiation was facilitated by the tendency of any language, even when uninfluenced by others, to develop in various respects differently in each area inhabited by a more or less isolated division of the heirs of its original speakers; and this tendency is likely to be intensified, almost beyond our imagining, in a preliterate age, when no written records exist to inhibit change. And note, in the preceding sentence, 'more or less': tribes *absolutely* isolated from *all* their 'kinsmen' will develop their common language differently, but so will tribes *relatively* isolated – separated, i.e., from the most distant of their kinsmen, but separated not by speakers of languages of different stocks, but rather by kinsmen speaking dialects intermediate between the two extremes. In such cases, the developing difference will tend to increase with the distance: dialect B will resemble dialect A in some ways and dialect C in others, D will resemble C in some ways and E in others, and so on. Now suppose that the speakers of dialects B, C, and D move out of their territories, which come to be occupied by their 'cousins' speaking dialects A and E, or that they become subject to the cultural and linguistic influence of those cousins; the result will be that the areas in which A and E are spoken will become contiguous, widely different though A and E may have come to be, and consequently that the single original language will *seem* to have developed very differently on the two sides of a sharp line. Precisely this process has occurred in historical times and is thoroughly documented: the Vulgar Latin of Paris, e.g., and the Vulgar Latin of Florence were originally separated by an indefinite number of varieties of Vulgar Latin shading into each other by almost imperceptible degrees. But gradually the language of Paris became standard south and east to the Italian border and the language of Florence north and west to the French border, with the result that the traveller in the Riviera suddenly finds, on crossing the border from France to Italy, that he must conduct his affairs in a very different language. There is every reason to believe that the same kind of thing happened in prehistoric times. 'East Germanic', e.g., resembles 'North Germanic' in some ways and 'West Germanic' in others. As this fact suggests, it was once spoken in intermediate territories. But its speakers moved away or were absorbed, and in the course of time their lands were filled up by speakers of North Germanic from the north and by speakers of West Germanic from the west (or rather from the south), who thus came face to face with languages more different from each other than mere geography would lead us to expect.

The result of all these circumstances promoting differentiation was that between, say, 3000 and 2000 B.C., the IE *language* had developed diversely into several IE *languages*, most of them mutually unintelligible, and spoken by peoples of whom some were widely separated and some near neighbours, but of whom almost all had lost or were to lose later all recollection of their common linguistic and cultural background.

Of the several main branches of the IE family, our earliest records, and hence our first direct evidences, are of very various dates, ranging from possibly as early as *c*. 1500 B.C. to as late as *c*. A.D. 1300. The several branches, furthermore, and the several members of these branches, have altered at very different rates and in very different degrees. These facts – and there are others that do likewise – complicate the analysis of the inter-relationships among the main branches of IE to such an extent that it is impossible to represent these relationships accurately in the form of a family tree: it is somewhat as if we were to try to draw up the genealogy of a very ancient and widespread human family some of whose members had died long before others, or left far fewer records of their existence, or inter-married with their distant cousins or with complete strangers much more or much less often, and much more or much less often in different generations. It is not a very great exaggeration to say that almost every main IE branch resembles almost every other more closely than it resembles the rest in this particular or that. The best we can do is to list the main branches in as nearly as possible the order of increasing difference – with the *caveat* that the interrelationship would be less well indicated graphically by a straight line than by a circle – and a circle both broken, and traversed by a network of chords.[1]

With this proviso, we may list the main IE branches and a specimen language or so for each, as follows (it matters little where we begin):

Germanic or Teutonic or Gothonic[2] (including English and German)

---

[1] The fact is that the familial or ancestral or genealogical analogy is decidedly imperfect: languages are not fathers and mothers, and do not beget or bear other languages. And yet that analogy is on the whole more useful and illuminating than any other that can conveniently be used.

[2] All three words are more or less commonly used, the first nowadays most commonly and the last least so. (1) *German(ic)* is of disputed origin. It probably applied at first to a particular Germanic tribe early known to the Romans, by whom it was later extended to the whole people (just as the earlier Romans extended the tribal name *Graeci* to the whole people calling themselves – as they still do – Hellenes). There seems to be little reason for identifying it, though there is a good deal of temptation to do so, with the Latin word *germanus* meaning 'fully akin', 'full kinsman', 'brother'. At any rate, it is hard to believe that many Romans did not make that identification. (2) *Teuton(ic)*. This is also in origin a tribal name (at least in late Roman use), and has been similarly extended to the whole people. It goes back to the same Germanic word for 'people' (*þeod* in the OE form) as has yielded the adjective *Dutch*, which originally meant practically 'popular'. *Teuton(ic)* certainly illustrates the tendency of a people to call themselves '*the* people', and *German(ic)* possibly illustrates a similar tendency for them to call themselves '(the) kinsmen'. (3) *Gothonic*. This neo-Latin word derives from Latin *Gothi*, *Got(h)ones*, *Gutones*, a name, originally, for yet a third specific Germanic tribe. More or less by accident it has never become applied so generally to the Germanic peoples as the two other names. It is also unlike them in being certainly a

Celtic (including Welsh, Irish, and Scottish Gaelic)
Italic (including Latin – and hence the Romance languages)
Hellenic (i.e., Greek)
{ Iranian (including modern Persian)
{ Indic (including ancient Sanskrit and modern Hindi)
{ Baltic (including Lithuanian)
{ Slavic (including Russian, Czech, and Polish)
(The braces indicate a specially close relation between Baltic and Slavic, and between Iranian and Indic.) There are at least four others (including Hittite, whose precise relation to IE is still disputed), but these eight are, in one way or another, the most important ones. Our knowledge of these branches, or at least of certain members of them, varies widely both in very quantity and in antiquity; some of the branches have more members, well- or little-known, and living or dead, than others, and they differ widely both in the number of members and in the degree of difference between those members. But one thing is certain: all the branches, including all the members, are, in structure and in the most ancient and fundamental parts of their vocabulary, nothing but variant forms of a single original language, viz., IE: the variations among them, essentially and fundamentally, are not different in kind, though they are sometimes amazingly different in degree, from the variations between the English of London and the English of New York.

The superficial differences between some of the branches are so vast that the underlying relationship hardly began to be realized, at least with any clarity or exactness, before the last quarter of the eighteenth century; and it was not until nearly a

true Germanic word for a specific Germanic people, probably meaning something like '(the people of) the inundated land' (with reference to the inundation of certain lands on the Baltic Sea some time before the Christian era). Of the three words, *Gothonic* is decidedly least commonly used, and *Germanic* almost as decidedly most commonly, though *Teutonic* was a close competitor till well within the twentieth century. The only trouble with *German(ic)* is that it is sometimes too easily understood with exclusive reference to the language and the inhabitants of what is now known as Germany; and consequently *Teutons* is occasionally found to be usefully clearer than *Germans*, and usefully more economical of space than 'Germanic peoples' or 'peoples speaking Germanic languages'.

century later that most of the principal details of correspondence
were understood. On the other hand, most of the principal details
are now understood – most of the principal formulae of correspondence and interrelation have now been established, and
established as rigorously as the leading facts, for example, of
palaeontology. A palaeontologist certainly does not know exactly
how a pterodactyl or a brontosaurus looked or exactly how they
are related to living reptiles or exactly how living reptiles are
related to each other, but just as certainly he has a pretty good
idea – an idea demonstrably much more likely to be near the
truth than the uninformed guess of the ordinary man. In precisely the same way, the student of the IE languages, prehistoric
and historic, living and dead, has a pretty good idea of their
interrelationships and of the general forms of some, at least,
of such of them as are unrecorded: his guess is a guess, if you
like, but an informed guess, and better than anyone else's: his
reconstruction of certain features of extinct and unrecorded IE
languages, including IE itself and, e.g., Primitive Germanic,
is an hypothesis, but a probable hypothesis, and much more
probable than any other. He is limited to saying, 'It *looks as if*
IE (or Primitive Germanic or prehistoric OE) had had such and
such features'; but it *does* 'look as if' it had had them, and not
some other set.

Just as we do not know exactly where all the Germanic
invaders of Britain were living immediately before the invasion,
so also we do not know where their ancestors (and the ancestors
of the Germanic peoples who remained on the Continent) lived
before the dawn of history, though the commonest opinion now
is that they lived on the southern and western coasts of the
Baltic Sea (where some of their descendants still live). It is also
disputed whether the most ancient 'Germans' removed at a comparatively early time from the centre of the belt of IE settlement,
or whether, on the contrary, they were, of all the IE peoples, the
'stay-at-homes'. What we do know is that at about the beginning
of the Christian era a large part of north-western Europe was
inhabited by speakers of tongues (Germanic) for the most part
mutually intelligible, that the speakers of those tongues then
enjoyed and for many centuries retained a sense of quasi-
national, (though certainly never, in historical times, political)

unity, and that English, or rather its Continental ancestor, was one of those tongues.

Our earliest records of the Germanic languages show a division, already of long standing, among what are called North, East, and West Germanic. North Germanic is equivalent to Scandinavian; East Germanic is equivalent for most practical purposes today to Gothic; West Germanic is everything else, including English. When we come to divide West Germanic, we find some difference of opinion, depending on the criteria selected by this or that student.[1] Briefly – and sufficiently for our present purposes – the difference resolves itself into whether we are to associate Dutch (and Flemish) and 'Low German' (*Plattdeutsch* – the provincial dialects of north-western Germany) with English, or, rather, with standard modern (High) German and the southern and south-eastern provincial dialects resembling it. If we select as our criterion of relationship certain prominent facts about certain sets of sounds, we shall classify Dutch, *Plattdeutsch*, etc., with English rather than with standard modern (High) German, and in any event, the difference, in this respect, between High German and all the rest is ancient, conspicuous, and important, and such as to set High German as much as a thousand years ago apart from the rest, which remained, till at least as late as that, on the whole mutually intelligible, however much more in common some of them may have had, by way of ancestry, with High German than with the others.

It would be interesting and by no means altogether irrelevant to consider here some of the details of these facts about Germanic sounds, but we could hardly do so without going far beyond the stated subject of this book, and much more deeply into phonetics – i.e., the science of speech sounds – than space will allow. But there is a very good reason for dealing with the subject of phonetics in part: chiefly the fact that, in our inspection of several versions of *St Luke* ii in the preceding chapter, though

[1] Considering the movements and mixtures of peoples, and the mysterious ways of linguistic change, it is not at all surprising that dialect B should resemble A in, e.g., sounds, and dialect C in vocabulary or some other feature. In such a case, obviously, the classification of B with A or C depends on the basis of classification.

we considered many differences among them, there was at least one very important one that we did not consider, viz., how they differed in sound. We could not and cannot consider that subject fruitfully without (1) some understanding of phonetics, and (2) some mutually intelligible way of stating phonetic facts.

Chapter IV

SOME ELEMENTS OF PHONETICS

★

IT IS easy to forget, or even not to realize, that language is
originally and primarily speech, not writing: that it is something heard before it is something seen. And even when it
becomes visible – i.e., when it gets written – the tendency of
speech to change, and the contrary tendency of writing (i.e.,
chiefly spelling) *not* to change, war against each other, and,
between them, almost always produce in the course of time an
increasing lack of correspondence between sound and symbol.
Generally speaking, the longer a language has been written, the
less exactly and intelligibly the spelling reflects the speech; and
the earlier the record we are trying to read, the more likely we
are to misinterpret what the spelling was meant to tell us of the
sounds.

For various reasons, this is true of English in a specially high
and even perhaps unique degree: such a degree that a reader of
an exposition of Early English pronunciation cannot possibly
form even a tolerably accurate notion of how (in the opinion of
the expositor) Early English sounded unless the expositor occasionally supplements conventional spelling with some kind of
phonetic transcription. A transcription based on the usual modern
'values' of the letters of the English alphabet is possible, but in
practice is inexact and ambiguous and misleading, and still, in
the end, nearly or quite as troublesome for the reader to learn
as a special alphabet – which has none of the countervailing
disadvantages. Accordingly, this chapter will set forth, as briefly
as is practical, the phonetic alphabet – substantially that of the
International Phonetic Association (henceforth IPA) – which will
be used in this book. But this alphabet will not be presented by
itself, or entirely in order to make possible the reader's understanding of the writer's statements about how Early English
sounded: along with it will go a brief introduction to phonetics.
The chief reason for including this subject is that pronunciation

changes gradually – which means that, however great and obvious
the difference between, say, an English sound of the twentieth
century and its 'ancestor' in the tenth, that difference is the
cumulative result of a long series of changes minute and each
at the moment unperceived. Now obviously, such a change must
be from one sound to another nearly – but not quite – like it;
and generally speaking, two sounds nearly alike are so because
they are produced by nearly – but not quite – the same means.
The means by which they are produced are of course the opera-
tions of the organs of speech; and without some notion of what
these organs are and how they operate, we can only dimly
understand how and why one sound comes gradually to take
the place of another. E.g., the prehistoric OE sound 'f' between
vowels became the historical OE sound 'v', and the NE sound
'ee' derives, most of the time, from (approximately) the ME
sound 'ay'. Without some understanding of how the organs of
speech produce sounds, such facts as these – and there are a
great many of them – remain mere facts: intelligible, in a way,
and memorizable, but isolated, apparently causeless and arbitrary,
and also – what is perhaps worse – subject to the suspicion that
they may not be facts at all. And yet they *are* facts, they can be
understood, and they are inherently interesting and instructive.

The division of the sounds of speech into vowels and consonants is familiar and useful and important, but in one way it
is not the most fundamental or illuminating division. That position is occupied by the division into 'voiced' and 'voiceless'
sounds. All vowels are voiced, but some consonants are voiced
and some voiceless.

What do we mean by 'voice'? In the immediately relevant and
confessedly somewhat technical sense, we mean the audible
vibrations of the vocal cords. The vibration is not only audible:
it is feelable. Place your finger-tips lightly on your Adam's apple
and say 'buzz' (prolonging the 'z'); you will feel a vibration as
long as you continue the 'z'. Now, keeping your fingers where
they were, say 'hiss', prolonging, this time, the 's'; you will feel
no vibration as long as you continue the 's'. *The only essential
difference* between the sounds of 'z' and 's' here is that 'voice' –
the vibration of the vocal cords – contributes a part of the first
sound but no part of the second.

All vowels are voiced;[1] i.e., all vowels owe part of their sound to the vibrating of the vocal cords. But so, we have just seen, do some consonants, and this fact raises two questions: (1) Wherein does the sound of 'z' *differ* from that of the vowel 'u' in 'buzz' or the vowel 'i' in 'hiss'? (2) Wherein does the *resemblance* of 'z' to 'u' or 'i' differ from its resemblance to 's'? The answer to the first question is that the sound of 'z' is contributed to not only by the vibration of the vocal cords but also by the audible friction of the breath passing through a narrow channel formed by the front of the tongue almost – but not quite – touching the palate just behind the teeth. The answer to the second question is that 'z', though like 'u' and 'i' and unlike 's' in having 'voice', is like 's' and unlike 'u' and 'i' in having audible friction.

'Z' and 's', then, are both consonants, but 'z' is a voiced consonant and 's' a voiceless one. But there are other consonants. 'D' and 't', e.g., are certainly consonants, and certainly similar; and a little observation will show (1) that they have nearly – but not quite – the same *point of articulation* (i.e., of contact or near contact between the operative organs – the front of the tongue and the part of the palate just behind the teeth, a part called the alveolus); and (2) that 'd' is to 't' what 'z' is to 's' (i.e., that 'd', like 'z', is voiced, and 't', like 's', voiceless). But there is a third point of difference: you can keep on saying 'z', 's', 'u', and 'i' as long as your breath holds out, but if you try to prolong 'd' or 't', you will find that you can't do it, and that, even if you seem to come near to doing it, all you actually succeed in doing is to introduce an interval of complete – and rather disconcerting – silence between starting the sound and finishing it. 'D' and 't', i.e., are not prolongable in the same sense as all the other sounds so far discussed are.

The reason for this is simple: in producing 'z' and 's', the tongue approaches the palate very nearly, but still leaves a narrow channel through which the breath continues to escape; in producing 'd' and 't', on the other hand, the tongue actually touches the palate for a moment and stops the breath, which shortly issues forth with an audible pop or click.

[1] In normal speech, i.e., not in whispering, which is a special case that we need not consider in this brief and general treatment.

We have here clearly a number of permutations and combinations, as follows:

Voice; *no* friction; *no* stoppage: 'u', 'i' (vowels).

Voice; friction; *no* stoppage: 'z' (voiced spirant).

Voice; *no* friction; stoppage: 'd' (voiced stop).

No voice; *no* friction; stoppage: 't' (voiceless stop).

No voice; friction; *no* stoppage: 's' (voiceless spirant).

Or, tabularly:

	Voice	*Friction*	*Stoppage*
'u', 'i'	*		
'z'	*	*	
'd'	*		*
't'			*
's'		*	

The names of these three kinds of sounds are reasonable: 'vowel' means 'vocalic', i.e., 'voiced' (and nothing else – nothing, i.e., of friction or stoppage); 'spirant' means 'breathing' (i.e., the friction of the breath passing through a channel above and beyond the vocal cords is audible); 'stop' means that the breath is momentarily and audibly stopped or checked.

Of the sounds already discussed, two present a difference that has not yet been commented on, viz., that between the sounds of 'u' in 'buzz' and 'i' in 'hiss'. Obviously they differ, and almost as obviously the difference does not consist in their being respectively prolongable and not prolongable (as 'z' and 's' differ from 'd' and 't') or in their respectively having or not having voice (as 'z' and 'd' differ from 's' and 't'). They differ chiefly because of the difference in the shape of the oral cavity[1] – a difference depending on the height to which the lower jaw is raised (i.e., how wide the mouth is open), the shape in which the lips are held (i.e., whether more or less rounded or more or less parallel), the part of the tongue raised nearest to the palate, and the height to which it is raised. The combined effect of all these modifications is to form 'resonance chambers' of different sizes and shapes, and the audible effect of these differences is the

[1] 'Mouth' would be less pretentious, but it is too likely to be misunderstood as 'lips'.

audible difference between, e.g., 'u' in 'buzz' and 'i' in 'hiss'. (A difference with an almost exactly similar cause chiefly accounts for the difference in 'tone' between, say, a horn and a trumpet playing in the same pitch at the same volume.)

Of the several determinants of such differences between various vowels, the part of the tongue nearest the palate and the degree of that nearness are, for several reasons, the most useful –or at least the most commonly used – to provide a basis for indicating the differences between the 'u' of 'buzz' and the 'i' of 'hiss' (and between other vowels differing in similar ways). In producing the 'i' of 'hiss', the front of the tongue is nearest (and very near) the palate, and we accordingly call this a *high front* vowel. For certain reasons, it would be confusing to describe at this point the 'u' of 'buzz' in comparable terms, so we will shift from it to the sound of 'u' in 'puss'. In producing the 'u' in 'puss', the *back* of the tongue is nearest (and very near) the palate, and we accordingly call *this* a *high back* vowel. Likewise the 'e' of 'men' is called a mid front vowel, the 'a' of 'man' low front, the 'o' of 'bone' mid back (but see further below under Diphthongs), and the 'a' of 'father' low back – all with reference to the relative height of what may be called (somewhat loosely) the operative part of the tongue.

So far we have spoken almost as if there were only six vowels: high front, mid front, low front, high back, mid back, and low back. Actually, however, this simple system is complicated by at least two facts, viz.: (1) Some vowels are neither front nor back, but what may be called central (i.e., neither the front nor the back of the tongue is conspicuously more elevated than the other); (2) some vowels differ from others neither in height nor in backness-or-frontness, but rather in 'length' or 'quantity' – i.e. (when these terms are strictly used), in literally taking a different length of time to pronounce: in being relatively prolonged or not prolonged. Let us look at these two facts in a little more detail.

(1) Central vowels may, like front and back ones, be high, mid, or low. For the limited purposes of this book, we may ignore the high central vowels, but we must mention some of the mid central and low central ones. NE, or rather that NE dialect called (among other things) 'Received Standard' (hence-

forth RS),[1] has three mid central vowels: (a) higher mid central
– the sound of 'a' in 'sofa', or of 'er' in 'offer' before a word (or
any following syllable) beginning with a consonant, or before
a pause: always unstressed: conventionally called 'schwa': the
commonest vowel in NE; (b) approximately the same sound
stressed, as in 'prefer' or 'err' (again, before a word, or any
following syllable, beginning with a consonant, or before a
pause); (c) lower mid central – the vowel of 'buzz'. (It will
perhaps begin to be apparent here why it was wise to shift
temporarily from 'buzz' to 'puss'.) The first of these mid central
vowels was in some surroundings even commoner in LOE and
ME than in NE; the second and third are peculiar to NE (i.e., as
against OE and ME – not as against all languages whatever).
Some dialects of NE have (and some dialects of LOE and ME
must have had) a low central vowel – about half-way between
the 'a' of 'hat' and the 'a' of 'father'.

(2) We are all used to talking about 'long' and 'short' vowels,
but we ordinarily use these terms in arbitrary and misleading
and historically accidental and phonetically inaccurate ways.
Thus we usually call the 'a' of 'hat' and the 'a' of 'hate' respectively 'short *a*' and 'long *a*', but, though the sounds are certainly
very different, the main difference is not essentially one of length
(or 'quantity') as the phonetician conceives length. Instead, the
'a' of 'hat' is low front; the 'a' of 'hate' is mid front (but see
further below under Diphthongs); neither is essentially 'longer'
than the other. Actual differences in length do occur in NE, but
they are almost always unconscious and automatic sequels or
accompaniments of other differences; generally (among stressed
vowels), a final vowel is long, one followed by a voiced consonant is 'half long', and one followed by a voiceless consonant
is short – 'a(y)' in 'hay' is long, in 'hayed' is half long, in 'hate'
short; and 'a' in 'had' (at least when the word is stressed) is
therefore actually longer than 'a' in 'hate'. Literal differences in
the length of vowels in NE, that is to say, are of little practical
importance and are seldom noticed. In OE and ME (as also in

[1] 'Received Standard' is probably the commonest name for what may be
called the dialect of most educated southern Englishmen – and, of course,
of many educated Englishmen in any part of the country, particularly those
educated at schools where RS is in general use.

many living languages) such differences *are* more or less important, in the sense that some words are distinguishable from each other only, or at least mainly, by the literal length of vowels, as they almost never are in NE. All this is unfortunately complicated by the fact that, when a vowel is literally long, it is likely to be 'abnormal' in other respects – likely, i.e., to be not only longer than the vowel most like it, but also louder (i.e., in effect, more strongly stressed), higher, and less central (i.e., more front if a front vowel, more back if a back one). Partly for more or less accidental historical reasons and partly because length is more independent of these concomitant qualities in ME – and still more in OE – than in NE, it is customary and often very useful to speak of OE and ME vowels as long and short, and to mark with a macron (ˉ) the letters designating 'long' vowel sounds in OE and sometimes ME words when they are not respelt phonetically; but even in OE and ME – especially ME – the so-called long and short vowels must often have differed more essentially and conspicuously in other ways than in literal length – chiefly in the long vowels' being *higher* than the short ones – and this is most decidedly true in NE.

There is one other often useful distinction among certain vowels, though we need not always mention it in describing them. This is whether the lips, when a vowel is pronounced, are relatively rounded or not. In most NE dialects, front vowels are never normally rounded; back vowels, on the other hand, normally are so in some noticeable degree. And the higher they are, the rounder; i.e., the high back vowel of 'who' is about as round as possible, the mid back vowel of 'hoe' (but see further below under Diphthongs) is less round, and the low back vowel of 'haw' is still less so. But note that it is rounder than the vowel of 'ha'. Both these vowels (that of 'haw' and that of 'ha') are called low back. That of 'haw' is not only rounder than that of 'ha' but also higher and more back, but in practice we usually need identify them respectively only as low back round and low back unround. The 'o' of 'pod' (in RS) is about half-way between the vowels of 'haw' and 'ha' in roundness, height, and 'backness'. Round front vowels, even though they do not ordinarily occur in NE, did occur in OE and ME, and we must accordingly take account of them. Anyone who has studied a little French or

German will be familiar with them. The round high front vowels are produced by placing the tongue as for the vowels of 'peel' and 'pill' and simultaneously rounding the lips as for those of 'pool' and 'pull'; the round mid front vowels, by placing the tongue as for the vowels of 'pale' and 'Pell' and simultaneously rounding the lips as for those of 'pole' and 'Paul'. We need not consider here the theoretical possibility of round low front vowels.

All the vowels so far discussed we may call (relatively) simple or single vowels. In most languages, there are other prominent vowel sounds that are essentially combinations, or rather sequences, of two vowels, but that are so frequent and, in apprehension, so unitary and individual, that we may often usefully regard them almost as if they were simple vowels. These are called diphthongs (or, when three vowels are involved, triphthongs). Of the two vowels composing a diphthong, either the first or the second is usually louder, i.e., more stressed, than the other; and it is usual, in NE, to restrict the name diphthong to sequences in which the first vowel is more stressed than the second. (These are called descending diphthongs, because the loudness 'descends', i.e., diminishes, from the first to the second sound.) Such diphthongs, in NE, are of two classes: (1) Those that everyone can recognize, in every NE dialect, as diphthongs; (2) those that, in at least some dialects, are less clearly, when at all, diphthongal – i.e., approach more nearly the quality of simple vowels. In class 1 belong the diphthongs of 'lied', 'loud', and 'Lloyd', which, despite the misleading spellings, are respectively (and approximately) (1) the first vowel of 'father' plus that of 'feed', (2) that of 'father' plus that of 'food', and (3) that of 'foam' plus that of 'feed'. In class 2 belong (1) the vowel of 'foam' itself, which in some dialects (notably RS) is not so much a simple mid back as mid back plus high back, and (2) the vowel of 'fame' or 'fade', which, in the same dialects, is not so much simple mid front as mid front plus high front. Of these five diphthongs, the fourth and fifth differ from the first three not only in being, in some NE dialects, less clearly diphthongal, by also in *having* been, in OE and ME, usually very *much* less clearly diphthongal, when diphthongal at all. It is chiefly for this latter reason that, in this book, which immediately deals with OE and ME rather than NE, the (approximate) vowel sounds of NE 'fame' and 'foam' are usually treated as simple vowels rather than as double ones, or diphthongs.

The distinction between vowels and consonants is not absolute; it hardly could be, considering what the organs of speech are and how they operate. Consequently we may expect to find border-line sounds – partly or sometimes vowels, and partly or sometimes consonants. We do indeed find them, and find them of more than one kind: (1) the 'y' in 'you' and the 'w' in 'we'; (2) 'n', 'm', and the sound spelt 'ng' in 'sing' (and 'n' in 'sink'); (3) 'l' and 'r'. Let us look briefly at each of these in turn.

(1) The 'y' in 'you' is virtually nothing but the 'ee' in 'bee' pronounced so briefly, and with the tongue so near the palate, and with so much more stress on the following vowel (and a vowel practically always follows), that the initial sound comes very close to that of 'sure' – comes very close, i.e., to being a consonant; the 'w' in 'we' has the same relation to the vowel in 'too'. These two sounds – 'y' in 'you' and 'w' in 'we' – are appropriately often called semi-vowels; they might at least equally well be called vocalic spirants. A still better name might be 'high vowels in consonant function'.

(2) Nasals. Stops are sounds made by *stopping* the breath *in the mouth* – either at the lips, or with the front of the tongue and the alveolus or teeth, or with the middle or back of the tongue and the palate. Nasals are made in the same ways, but differ greatly in auditory effect because the breath, though stopped in the mouth, is released through the nose. This is made possible by opening the flap that usually closes off the nasal cavity from the oral, with the result that nasal sounds are characterized by the peculiar resonance of the nasal cavity. There are three clearly distinct nasals: (a) 'n', produced by the front of the tongue against the backs of the upper front teeth ('dental nasal') or against the alveolus, the part of the palate just above and behind the teeth ('alveolar nasal'); in NE, at least, if not in OE and ME, the second variety (the alveolar) is usual, but it is none the less often called dental (since true dentals are commoner, in languages generally, than alveolars, and since a single language seldom contains both); (b) 'm', a nasal produced by pressing the lips together ('labial nasal'); (c) the final sound of 'sing' – spelt in this word with two letters, but really just as

much a single and distinct sound as 'n' and 'm'; produced by contact between the back of the tongue and the soft palate, or 'velum' (hence called the 'velar nasal'); an almost indistinguishable 'relative' of this sound, and one not usually worth distinguishing from it, is produced a little further forward in the mouth, in which case the sound is called the 'palatal nasal'. Note here especially that the usual NE spelling is ambiguous: in 'singer', 'ng' stands for the velar (or palatal) nasal alone; in 'finger', 'ng' stands for that nasal plus the velar (or palatal) voiced stop. In OE and ME, 'ng' seems usually to have meant what it means in NE 'finger' rather than in NE 'singer'. In NE often, and in OE and ME sometimes, the first and second of these three nasals – 'n' and 'm' – become practically vowels. All that is meant by this is that, whatever the spelling, these sounds sometimes act by themselves as syllables, as in the second syllable of 'bottom' and 'cotton'. Nasals are sometimes associated with vowels in another way. During the pronunciation of a vowel, the passage between the oral and nasal cavities may be opened *without* any closure's being made in the mouth, with the result, naturally, that the vowel sound issues from the mouth and the nose together, and combines the resonances of both. Such a vowel is sensibly called a nasalized vowel. Nasalized vowels are only accidental and unconscious in NE, but some of them must be recognized as distinct sounds in some periods of OE, and in many other languages, notably and familiarly French. The tendency is for a nasalized vowel not only to be nasalized, but also (for certain physiological reasons) to be, in terms of the position of the tongue, lower than the vowel before it was nasalized, or more back, or both. Thus French *i* unnasalized is high front; nasalized, it becomes low front.

(3) Two other sounds are also sometimes rather consonants than vowels and at other times rather vowels than consonants, viz., 'r' and 'l'. They are conveniently, however unscientifically, called liquids. 'L' is produced with the tongue touching the palate at about the same place as for 'd' and 't', but with the sides of the tongue lowered so as to let the breath (and the sound) pass through. 'Little' illustrates both the consonantal function of 'l' (in the first sound of the word) and the vocalic (in the last). What the letter 'r' represents is harder to define.

It is hard because there are so many different kinds of *r*. The one that is both most familiar to speakers of RS and perhaps closest to what might be called 'standard *r*' is the one usually heard before a vowel, especially a stressed one, as in 'raid'. Its point of articulation is nearly that of the initial sound of 'sure'. There are other kinds of *r*: one, common in Scotland, has about the same articulation, but involves a louder and longer 'trilling' of the front of the tongue; another trilled, or rather 'rolled', *r*, the 'Northumbrian burr', and common also in some kinds of French and German, is articulated between the back of the tongue and the uvula (the little pink tag or flap hanging down from the back of the soft palate over the back of the tongue) and is accordingly called the uvular *r*. In RS, where 'r' occurs in the spelling after a vowel, it is commonly not pronounced at all unless it is also followed by a vowel; but in many other varieties of NE, including those spoken by most Americans, it *is* pronounced – but pronounced often less as a consonant (voiced spirant) than as a vague, obscure vowel which somehow resembles the consonant *r*, and which is accordingly called an '*r*-coloured' vowel. In these kinds of NE, this *r*-coloured vowel occurs independently in the pronunciation of, e.g., the second syllable of 'offer'. Most southern Englishmen pronounce here, the same sound, but without the *r*-colouring (except before a vowel) – i.e., they pronounce a schwa. To put it another way, for a speaker of RS 'dater' and 'data' (except before vowels) are identical in sound; for most Americans (and many Britons) they are not. In this respect, OE and ME seem to have agreed more nearly with (western) American NE than with RS.

Here let us return to pure consonants (i.e., those that never serve nearly or quite as vowels). We have seen that there are two kinds of such consonants: spirants ('z' in 'buzz', 's' in 'hiss') and stops ('d' and 't'). We have also seen that all four of these sounds have nearly the same point of articulation, and that they are all therefore called alveolars (though 'd' and 't' are sometimes called dentals because that is what they are in most other languages than English). There are other such sets of sounds differing essentially from these only in their point of articulation. Thus just as 'z', 's', 'd', 't' (and 'n') are alveolars, so the first sound of 'sure' or 'shore' and the second of 'azure' are postalveolars (i.e., formed by the tongue's approaching the palate a little further back than for 'z' and 's'); what are spelt 'th' (both the sound in 'then' and that in 'thin') are linguo-dentals (formed by the tongue against the upper front teeth); 'b' and 'p' are labials (formed by pressing the lips together, as 'm' is); 'v' and 'f' are labio-dentals (formed by the upper teeth against the lower lip); and 'k' (or 'hard *c*') and 'hard *g*' are palatals (usually before or after front vowels) or velars (usually before or after back vowels), like what is usually spelt 'ng' as in 'sing' and 'song'. All these, it is important to note, occur in pairs – voiced and voiceless – just as 'z' and 's', 'd' and 't' do; and some are spirants, like 'z' and 's', and some stops, like 'd' and 't'. But there is one voiceless spirant frequent in NE (and OE, ME, and most languages), viz., 'h', which may, for the limited purposes of this book, be regarded as having no voiced or stopped correlatives. (A convenient name for spirants like 'z', 's', 'h', 'th', 'sh' is *fricatives* – i.e., 'rubbing sounds' – to distinguish them from the semi-vowels, the nasals, and the liquids, all of which, as we have seen, though mainly spirants, are nearly or sometimes vowels.)

These are all the stops and spirants ordinarily and consciously used in RS and in most other NE dialects, but there are two other spirants (specifically fricatives) that must be mentioned because they occur in OE or ME (or some NE dialects) and enter into the history of certain sound changes. They are (1) the (voiceless) sound spelt 'ch' in Scots 'loch' or German 'ich' and 'ach' (the fricative with the same point of articulation as the stop 'k'); (2) the same sound voiced (more or less as in emitting the 'sound of disgust', 'ugh!').

Finally, before we leave stops and fricatives we must mention two combinations, each of a stop plus a fricative, but each often apprehended as, and actually sometimes 'behaving' more or less like, a single sound. These differ from each other only in that one is voiceless and the other voiced. They are (voiceless) the sound heard at both the beginning and the end of 'church', and (voiced) that at both beginning and end of 'judge'. The voiceless sound is (almost but not quite) 't' plus the sound usually spelt 'sh'; the voiced, almost but not quite 'd' plus the second sound of 'azure'. (We must say 'not quite' 't' and 'd' here because, in producing the sounds, the tongue touches the palate a little behind the position for independent 't' and 'd'; touches it, i.e., at the same point as it approaches for the following fricatives. But for the purposes of practical transcription, this quasi-'t' and this quasi-'d' are treated as regular 't' and 'd'.) Such an intimate union of a stop and a fricative has the special name of *affricate*. There are others in other languages, but these two are the only ones we need normally consider in English.

We began this chapter by observing that letters do not always indicate the same sounds as they indicated in OE and ME and that consequently we can hardly understand discussions of OE and ME pronunciation without a phonetic transcription. The reader of the intervening pages must several times have been reminded of the familiar but easily forgotten fact that even within NE the same letters do not always indicate the same sounds (e.g., 'a' in 'hat', 'hate', (RS) 'half', and 'hall'; 'ng' in 'singer' and 'finger', 'th' in 'then' and 'thin'), that the same sounds are not always indicated by the same letters (e.g., 'fay', 'fait', 'fate', 'fête'), that some simple sounds are often – but not always! – confusingly spelt with two letters (cf. '*sh*ore' and '*s*ure', '*j*udge' and 'ju*dge*'), that some double sounds are often just as misleadingly spelt with one letter (e.g., the pronoun 'I'), and finally that NE dialects differ in their interpretation of letters. And we should also remember the plague of 'silent letters' in NE: most final *e*'s, the 'k' in 'know', the 'w' in 'wrong', the 'gh' in 'night'. All these considerations should make it clear that in order to discuss comfortably the pronunciation of the English of any period we must, in practice, adopt both a phonetic transcription, and not one based on the present use of the alphabet in English, but rather one with the fundamental principle of one letter for each sound and one sound for each letter – and no silent letters. The transcription presented below and used in this book is an adaptation, as has been said before, of the phonetic alphabet of the International Phonetic Association (IPA). The sounds we need to represent (there are, of course, in language at large a great many more, and we are furthermore disregarding comparatively minute and – for our purposes – unimportant variations even within NE) are designated, classified, arranged, and described for the most part in the terms used in the foregoing pages.

(A vacant place in the table indicates, not necessarily that the sound that would logically occupy it does not exist, but that for one reason or another it need not be included here. Here, *as everywhere else in this book,* PHONETIC SYMBOLS ARE ENCLOSED IN SQUARE BRACKETS.)

Vowels

		Unround		Round	
		As	*And*	*As*	*And*
Tongue		*pronounced*	*symbolized*	*pronounced*	*symbolized*
placement		*in*	*by*	*in*	*by*
Higher high front		*peel*	[i]	Germ. *Hüte,*	[y]
				Fr. *du*	
Lower high front		*pill*	[ɪ]	Germ. *Hütte*	[Y]
Higher mid front		*pale*	[e]*	Germ. *schön,*	[ɸ]
				Fr. *peu*	
Lower mid front (long)			[ɛ:]		
Lower mid front (short)		*Pell*	[ɛ]	Germ. *können,*	[œ]
				Fr. *neuf*	
Higher low front		*pair* (RS)	[æ:]		
Lower low front		*pal*	[æ]		
Higher mid central (stressed)		*prefer* (RS)	[ɜ]**		
Higher mid central (unstressed)		*offer* (RS), so-*fa* ('schwa')	[ə]**		
Lower mid central		*but*	[ʌ]		
Low central			[a]		
Higher high back				*pool*	[u]
Lower high back				*pull*	[ʊ]
Mid back				*pole*	[o]*
Higher low back (round)				*Paul*	[ɔ]***
Lower low back (round)				*pod* (RS)	[ɒ]***
Low back (unround) (long)		*bah!*	[ɑ:]		
Low back (unround) (short)		*father*	[ɑ]		

Diphthongs

Tongue placement	*As pronounced in*	*And symbolized by*
Low back unround plus high front	*lied*	[ɑi]****
Low back unround plus high back	*loud*	[ɑu]****
Mid back plus high front	*Lloyd*	[ɔi]****

Semi-vowels

High front (consonantal *i*)	*you, yoke*	[j]
High back (consonantal *u*)	*we, woke*	[w]

Nasals

Articulation		
Labial consonantal	*mail, lame*	[m]
Labial vocalic	*bottom*	[m̩]
Alveolar ('dental') consonantal	*nail, lane*	[n]
Alveolar ('dental') vocalic	*cotton*	[n̩]
Velar or palatal (consonantal only)	*song, singer*	[ŋ]

Liquids

Alveolar consonantal	*little* (first *l*)	[l̩]
Alveolar vocalic	*little* (second *l*)	[l̩]
Post-alveolar consonantal	*raid*	[r]
Post-alveolar vocalic (rare in RS)	*better*	[r̩]

Pure Consonants

	Stops				Fricatives			
	Voiceless		Voiced		Voiceless		Voiced	
Articulation	*as in*	*Symbol*	*as in*	*Symbol*	*as in*	*Symbol*	*as in*	*Symbol*
Labial	*pail*	[p]	*bail*	[b]				
Labio-dental					*fail*	[f]	*vail*	[v]
Linguo-dental					*thin*	[θ]	*then*	[ð]
Alveolar ('dental')	*tail*	[t]	*dale*	[d]	*lice*	[s]	*lies*	[z]
Post-alveolar					*assure*	[ʃ]	*azure*	[ʒ]
Velar (or palatal)	*coal, kin*	[k]	*goal, begin*	[g]	Germ. *ach, ich*	[x]	*ugh!*	[ɣ]
Glottal					*hail*	[h]		

Affricates

The two affricates that must commonly be taken into account in English are the consonant sounds in *church* (voiceless) (transcribed [tʃ]) and *judge* (voiced) (transcribed [dʒ]). The articulation of both is post-alveolar.

Additional Symbols

['] before a syllable(or sometimes the first element oι a diphthong) denotes primary (often the only) stress; [ˌ], a secondary one when there is one that it is useful to designate. [:] is occasionally used after a vowel symbol to indicate exceptional length (often accompanied by, and even mainly consisting in, exceptional height or loudness or both) of vowels whose symbols do not ordinarily include it. [˜] over a vowel indicates nasalization.

Notes

* Warning has already been given that these sounds in RS NE are rather [ei] and [ou].
** The IPA properly provides separate symbols for the 'r-coloured' varieties of these sounds, but this book, to avoid unnecessary complications, will use instead [ɜr] and [ər] (or [r̩]). Convenience is also sometimes served by writing [əm] and [ən] instead of [m̩] and [n̩].
*** It would be more conventional to symbolize these sounds by [ɔ:] and [ɔ] respectively, but for the purposes of this book the usages here indicated seem more practical.
**** Both elements of these transcriptions are only approximations, but the transcriptions are those in common use and quite sufficiently accurate for the purposes of this book.

Chapter V

HOW OLD ENGLISH SOUNDED AND HOW IT WAS SPELT

★

WE MAY now discuss, with some hope of understanding, how OE sounded, but we must still confront some difficulties. In the first place, how confidently can we make even the most general statements about how any language heard by no living man sounded?[1]

The answer, at least in the case of Early English, is, 'pretty confidently so long as pretty generally'. It is undoubtedly true that King Alfred, say, would find the modern students' pronunciation of his preface to the OE translation of St Gregory's *Pastoral Care* uncouth, but it is also undoubtedly true that he would understand it, whereas he quite certainly would not understand a pronunciation interpreting OE spelling according to the usual 'values' of the letters in NE spelling. The opening sentence of that preface, in the Bodleian ms Hatton 20, runs as follows (when printed in the modern fashion): 'Ælfrēd kyning[2]

---

[1] It is bemusing to consider how the invention of the phonograph may affect our descendants' knowledge of our speech, but even more to consider how that same invention may affect the development of speech itself. Given the continuance of our present technology, we shall certainly leave to our descendants a perfect record of our speech, as no generation has done before; but that very record will almost certainly inhibit further change, and thus technology will, in a sense, defeat one of its own ends. One could almost wish that King Alfred had invented the phonograph, made records, and buried them – that the invention had then been forgotten, and the phonograph ceased to be used – and that it had been subsequently reinvented, and the records discovered.

[2] This word is more normally spelt *cyning*; if it happened to be so here, a modern Englishman would naturally pronounce it even more differently – ['sɑinɪŋ] – from King Alfred's pronunciation than is indicated in the transcription below.

hāteð grētan Wærferð biscep his wordum luflīce ond frēondlīce.'[1]
A literate modern southern Englishman acquainted of course
with these conventional NE 'values' (and attending to the macrons,
or 'long marks') but unacquainted with any of the OE orthographical conventions except that þ and ð equal NE *th* (i.e., [θ]
and [ð]) would pronounce the passage about as follows: [ˈiilfrid
ˈkainıŋ ˈhetıθ ˈgritn ˈwiəfəθ ˈbisəp hız ˈwədm̩ ˈlʌflais ɒnd
ˈfriəndlais]. King Alfred, on the other hand, would theoretically
– and very probably – have pronounced it about as follows:
[ˈælvred[2] ˈkynıŋ(g) ˈhɑ:tɛθ ˈgre:tan ˈwærvɛrθ ˈbiʃɛp hıs
ˈwɒrdʊm ˈlʊvlitʃɛ ɒnd ˈfreɒndlitʃɛ].

A comparison of the two phonetic transcriptions will show
that what we may call the naïve NE pronunciation exactly
corresponds with King Alfred's theoretical pronunciation in only
two syllables – the second of *kyning*, and *ond* – out of twenty-
two (if *luflīce* and *frēondlīce* are given three syllables, according
to the OE – twenty if they are given two, according to the NE).
The second transcription almost certainly only approximates
King Alfred's pronunciation, but, with virtually equal certainty,
it *does* approximate it, whereas the first transcription indicates a
pronunciation so different from his that it would be unintelligible
to him.

What reason have scholars for saying with such confidence as
they do that the second transcription of the passage is very close
to representing, and the first very far from representing, King
Alfred's pronunciation?

To answer this question at the same time briefly and completely is impossible, and to try to answer it completely –
whether briefly or not – would be out of place in such a book as
this. Such answer as is given below applies as a whole, furthermore, to reconstructing the pronunciation of extinct languages

---

[1] 'King Alfred commands [me, his secretary,] to greet Bishop Wærferth
with his compliments in loving and friendly fashion.'

[2] Note that the NE pronunciation with [f] instead of [v] is a modern
spelling pronunciation, not a normal continuous development from spoken
OE. While the OE tradition was still alive, *Alfred* was often spelt (in EME)
'alured' (i.e., with 'u' meaning 'v', 'alvred'). In modern times, incidentally,
this ME use of 'u' for 'v' led, quaintly enough, to the pronunciation
[æljurɛd].

generally; only some parts of it are certainly applicable, and still fewer uniquely applicable, to the special case of OE.

Hypotheses about how extinct languages sounded are approximately on a level with hypotheses about how extinct animals which have left fossil skeletons looked. In both cases, informed students agree, and agree within fairly narrow limits, though they sometimes disagree on fairly large details, and are almost always unwilling to be dogmatic about small ones. The several principal kinds of evidence on which philologists depend in reconstructing an extinct pronunciation are as follows : (1) Early writers' descriptions of how certain sounds were articulated. If, e.g., a Sanskrit grammarian of many centuries ago describes a sound as articulated by the edges of the upper front teeth and the lower lip, we cannot doubt that he was describing [f] or [v]. (2) Transliteration from one alphabet to another, and phonetic representations of loan-words. E.g., Latin *uictor* was transliterated into Greek ουίκτωρ (ūictōr); if Latin *u* (con-sonant) had not still been [w] instead of [v] as it later became, the Greeks would pretty certainly have transliterated it other-wise. Again, Latin *Caesar* (where *C* indicates [s] in NE) is found in EOE as *casere* ['kɑ:zɛrɛ], whereas, had Latin *c* already changed from [k] to [s], the OE form would certainly have been spelt, say, **sasere* or the like. (3) The rather remarkably stable and persistent school tradition of Latin spelling. E.g., Latin *Iouem* ['jɒwɛm] develops regularly, in Italian, into [dʒovɛ], and is accordingly spelt *Giove* in Italian; but even Italians seem, century after century, to have continued to pronounce the initial *i* as [j] in a Latin context instead of making the popular change to [dʒ]; indeed, otherwise they would not have devised the newfangled spelling *gi* for [dʒ]. (It must be admitted that they did, how-ever, change the value of consonant *u* from [w] to [v] in pronouncing Latin just as they did in their vernacular.) (4) In the special case of NE, we find that the sounds designated by the 'long' vowel letters (ā, ē, ī, ō, ū, ȳ) are almost all of them different from those designated pretty consistently in all the other modern languages using the Roman alphabet. Confronted with this fact, we must suppose *either* (a) that English has always used different values; *or* (b) that the NE values are the original universal values, that English has not changed, and that all the other languages not only have changed, but have changed in approximately the same way; *or* (c) that English alone has changed. Obviously, the third hypothesis is almost infinitely more probable than either of the others. (5) Foreigners' uninstructed or 'phonetic' spelling of English. E.g., seventeenth-century Frenchmen, when telling their countrymen how to pronounce English, usually spell *pale* as *péle* ([ˈpel] or [pɛːl]). Again, Frenchmen of five or six centuries earlier, when they start writing English words, consistently write *child* and *cold* (or *cald*), whereas their Anglo-Saxon contemporaries just as consistently write *cild* and *cald* – a clear indication that the initial sounds of the two words had once been at least virtually identical, that they had come to be decidedly different, and that the native English were not in the habit of showing the difference in the spelling. (6) When one sound replaces another in the received pronunciation of a language, the new sound (a) develops gradually and unconsciously, not suddenly and deliberately, and (b), largely, for just that reason, is, at least in its early stages, a sound articulated at nearly the same place and in nearly the same way as the old one. E.g., in NE *I*, the present sound, [ˈɑi], is very different from the original one, [iː]; it is a diphthong, not a monophthong, and the first element is a low back vowel, not a high front one. But the development must clearly have begun with [əˈi] i.e., the original sound preceded by a faint and unstressed (and unconscious) schwa – and have proceeded through some such stages as [ˈəi] (shift of stress), [ˈʌi], [ˈɑi]. (7) This kind of sequence is one of many reflections of what is called the phonetic drift of a language – the general direction in which its sounds tend to develop over the centuries. E.g., [k] before a front vowel tends generally – or at least tended in Vulgar Latin in the early Christian centuries – itself to be fronted, i.e., to be articulated by a further and further forward part of the tongue touching a further and further forward part of the palate. This is so natural as to be almost inevitable in the absence of inhibiting factors – instinctive laziness leads the tongue to anticipate, in articulating the consonant, the articulation of the following vowel, so as to avoid an abrupt and violent shift in position. Today most of the Romance languages (a) reflect this fronting, (b) carry the process further than a mere fronting, and (c) carry

it to different places. Latin *centum* was pronounced [ˈkɛntum].
In Italian this becomes [ˈtʃɛnto], in Spanish [ˈθjɛnto], in French
[sã]. All three reflexes[1] of [k] are, so to speak, different exten-
sions of the 'curve' from a velar or back [k] to a palatal or front
one; the tongue, having progressed from the velum to a more
forward part of the palate, continues its wanderings along somewhat different paths, all of which arrive at points and modes of
articulation that facilitate, in different ways, the transition from
the (originally back) consonant to the following front vowel.

We may go at this from the opposite direction. *Cento*
[ˈtʃɛnto], *ciento* [ˈθjɛnto], and *cent* [sã] have obviously a common 'ancestor'; the question is how we know how that common
ancestor, *centum*, was pronounced. Now if the sound denoted by
ancient Latin *c* had been [s] or some other front fricative or
affricate, we should expect speakers of each of the Romance
languages respectively to pronounce *all* its reflexes of Latin *c*
with a single (front fricative or affricate) sound; but in fact
they pronounce these reflexes with such a sound only when the
following vowel in Latin was *e*, *i*, or *y*, whereas, when the
following vowel was *a*, *o*, or *u*, Italian and Spanish have [k];
e.g., Latin *carum* yields Italian and Spanish *caro* [ˈkɑːro]. (The
situation in French is more complex and not worth going into
here, but it supports essentially the same conclusion.) Now
there is certainly anything but a difficulty in supposing that,
when Italian and Spanish have [k], Latin had it also; and when
we further observe (a) that, even when Italian and Spanish
have a front fricative or affricate, they still use the *c* spelling,
(b) that we have every reason to believe that Latin spelling
was reasonably 'phonetic' and consistent, and (c) that the Italian,
Spanish, and French sounds of *c* before a front vowel ([tʃ], [θ],
and [s]) can all be best explained as – can hardly be explained
otherwise than as – various developments from [k]: when we
observe and consider all these things, we end with the almost
inevitable conclusion that the several Romance sounds all go
back to a single ancient Latin sound different from all of them –
and practically identical with the sound that Italian and Spanish

[1] Reflexes – sounds (or forms) developing from earlier ones; e.g., the
normal NE reflex of OE [ɑː] is [o] (or [ou]), as in NE *bone* [bo(u)n]
reflecting OE *bān* [bɑːn].

preserve before a back vowel. In short, the hypothesis that Latin *centum* was pronounced [ˈkɛntum] is only an hypothesis, indeed, but it is all but infinitely the most probable hypothesis: it is, all things considered, much the best 'guess', and is all but demonstrably right. (8) Illiterate spellings. This is closely related to point 5 above, and in some degree to point 2. A more or less professional or constant writer tends to follow the spelling conventions of the books he knows, whereas his contemporary who is, like Bill Stumps, 'little in the habit of original composition', tends to spell according to his notions of a phonetic system – notions tempered by such deference to the conventional orthography as he can exhibit. Thus when, in LOE, *ie* and *y* are constantly confused, it is clear that the sounds [ɪə] and [ʏ] (and [iə] and [yː]) had, in the writer's dialect, fallen together; or when, in the seventeenth century, the steward – or the lady, or even the lord – of a manor writes 'itarnle' for *eternal,* it is clear that the writer rhymed the second syllable with *barn* rather than with *burn*. (Note, incidentally, the preservation of this type of pronunciation in the present RS pronunciation of *sergeant* and *clerk* and *Derby* and in the slang *varsity*.) (9) Rhyme. From this source we can learn almost nothing about OE, but a good deal about ME and ENE. It is of little use to us with OE because OE verse almost never uses rhyme; it is of a good deal of use to us with ME and ENE because verse in those periods (a) *does* use rhyme, and (b) seldom or never uses 'eye-rhymes'.[1] Eye-rhymes can hardly have become common before the seventeenth century or even the eighteenth; for, until nearly that period, most English and other European vernacular verse was designed – or was at least modelled on verse designed – to be *heard* by many more people than it was designed to be read silently and privately by, and spelling, furthermore, was a good deal more flexible than it is now and a good deal less regarded as determining rather than reflecting the sound. Consequently, when we get what look to us like imperfect rhymes in an age when eye-rhymes were beginning to be possible, we have the best conceivable evidence as to sound – as in Pope's rhyming *besieg'd* and *oblig'd* (both certainly [-iːdʒd]), or *join* and *divine* (both [-ʌin] or the like),

---

[1] Eye-rhymes – 'rhymes' that are so, in the pronunciation of the rhymer, only to the eye, not to the ear – e.g., *to, go*.

or *obey* and *tea* (both [-e]). (10) Alliteration. This, rather than rhyme, is the structural principle of OE verse, and of much of ME. The rules of its practice require ordinarily at least two alliterating stressed syllables in a four-stressed line. When we find a ME alliterative poet writing a line in which the only possible alliterating stressed syllables begin respectively with *wh* and *qu*, we can be morally certain that these were on occasion for him (or at least for the copyist of the extant ms or of some antecedent one) ways of spelling the same sound, and that accordingly the two words, despite the variant spellings, at any rate sometimes had the same or at least what passed for the same initial sound.

By a careful comparison and counterbalancing of these kinds of evidence, philologists arrive at theories of approximately how extinct languages sounded. Individual students differ on details, but they are in substantial agreement about the main outlines, and therein lies the principal claim of those main outlines to being accepted as generally correct. It is true that some pieces of the jig-saw puzzle are missing, that some have had their edges worn away, that we even have sometimes different pieces from slightly different puzzles, and that it is unwise – and unusual – to be dogmatic about which piece one should begin with; but in the end, all triers come out with very nearly the same disposition of pieces, and with a picture clearly more intelligible and credible than any alternative.

Let us now see what they have come out with in OE. Below are set forth the letters of the OE alphabet, with the values that they are now usually thought to have had in the West Saxon of the tenth century.

CONSONANTS

b, d, k, l, m, n, p, q, t, w, x, and *z* (of which *k, q,* and *z* were seldom used) had the same value as they usually have in NE.

r was never 'silent' or 'dropped'.

h was just that initially; medially before consonants, and finally, it was [x], as in *niht* ('night'), [nixt], and *seah* ('saw', verb), ['sæəx]. (Earlier it was that everywhere; just when it became [h] initially, no one can say.)

c and *g* may best be dealt with more or less together. OE *c* was (in native words) descended from what was at first identical in sound with Germanic [k], the voiceless velar or palatal stop; OE *g* was (in most[1] native words) descended from Germanic [ɣ], the voiced velar fricative. In OE, both *c* and *g* developed according to the general tendency to facilitate speech by assimilating one of two successive sounds to the other. *c* and *g* having had two parallel developments, and *g* having had one to itself, it will be well to despatch first the development peculiar to *g*. This development consisted in a change from the voiced velar fricative [ɣ] to the voiced velar stop [g], and occurred (1) initially before back vowels and (2) everywhere before consonants. (Whether this happened as early as the tenth century is uncertain, but it had certainly happened by the time of the Norman Conquest.) The two other developments of [k] and [ɣ] are exactly parallel: (1) With the exception just noted for [ɣ], both remained as they had been, in the neighbourhood of back vowels (as is natural, considering that both were back consonants to begin with); (2) both became fronted (respectively to [tʃ] and [j]) in the neighbourhood and through the influence of front vowels – as is equally natural. E.g., *cōm* ('came') [koːm], and *dagas* ('days'), ['daɣas], retained their [k] and [ɣ] unchanged; but *cild* ('child') at first (kild], became eventually [tʃild], and likewise *gester* ('yester-'), at first ['ɣɛstər], became eventually ['jɛstr]: in both words the initial back consonants were so to speak pushed forward by the following front vowels so as to make the transition easier. (If you will try producing [k] and [ɣ] further and further forward in the mouth, you will probably find that you end – as the late Anglo-Saxons did – with approximately [tʃ] and [j].)[2]

---

[1] A few instances of OE *g* are descended from Germanic [j], and never designated anything but [j], but they *are* few.

[2] There are a good many apparent exceptions to the generalization that these two sounds were fronted in the neighbourhood and through the influence of front vowels. E.g., *cēlan* ('keel', as in 'Greasy Joan doth *keel* the pot'), ['keːlan], not ['tʃeːlan]: and *gyldan* ('gild'), ['ɡyldan], not ['jyldan]. The explanation is that, by at least the tenth century, *y* and *ȳ* always, and *e* and *ē* often, in what we may call 'classical' West Saxon spelling, represent vowel sounds that, though by that time front, had developed, under special conditions, out of vowel sounds originally back. An

cg. This digraph had come, at least by the eleventh century, to stand for [dʒ]; e.g., *hecg*, 'hedge', [hedʒ].

sc. This digraph at first everywhere represented [sk], just as *c* at first everywhere represented [k]; but whereas *c* continued to represent [k] only in some situations, and came to represent [tʃ] in others, *sc* came to represent [ʃ] almost everywhere; e.g., not only *scip* ('ship'), [ʃɪp], but also *sc(e)adu* ('shade'), [ˈʃ(j)adu], and *scrūd* ('shroud', 'garment'), [ʃruːd]. It is not very clear why [sk] should have been fronted more generally than [k] alone, but it appears to have been so.

f, þ (ð), and *s.* These letters, in tenth-century OE, represented voiceless fricatives always when doubled, and also when single unless they were *both preceded and followed* by voiced sounds; i.e., they represented respectively [f], [θ], and [s] initially[1] and finally, and also medially unless they were both preceded and followed by a vowel or a voiced consonant, in which case they represented the voiced correlatives, i.e., [v], [ð], and [z], of the same sounds. For various reasons, OE inherited few voiced fricatives from Germanic, but it developed some out of voiceless

understanding of these special conditions affords an illuminating and characteristic example of how and why, sometimes, sounds change. Prehistoric OE had an adjective **cōl* ('cool'), pronounced [koːl], and a related verb **cōljan* ('to make cool'), pronounced [ˈkoljɑn]. The [j] of [ˈkoljɑn] was a high front sound, and tended, before its ultimate disappearance, to front (indirectly) the preceding [o] to [ø], which was later unrounded to [e], whence [ˈkeːlɑn]; whereas the [o] of [koːl], having nothing to front it, remained a back (and round) vowel. Similarly, Prehistoric OE had a noun **guld* ('gold'), pronounced [ˈɣuld], and a related verb **guldjan* ('to cover a surface with gold'), pronounced [ˈɣuldjɑn]. The high front [j] of [ˈɣuldjɑn] tended, before disappearing, to front (indirectly) the preceding [u] to [y], whence *gyldan* [ˈɣyldɑn], later [ˈgyldɑn]; whereas the [u] of **guld*, having nothing to front it, remained a back vowel. (The later lowering of **guld* [ɣuld] to *gold* [gɒld], the still later unrounding of *gyld-* [gyld] to *gild-* [gɪld], and the even later 'lengthening' and raising of [gɒld] to [gold] are matters that we cannot properly go in to here.)

[1] There is some reason to believe that these letters, when initial, represented voiced sounds (i.e., [v], [ð], and [z]) in West Saxon of the tenth century, but they were certainly voiceless – [f], [θ], and [s] – in that position in Mercian, which is the 'ancestor' of standard NE.

fricatives in the course of time, and developed them in exactly the places and for exactly the reasons that we might expect: viz., near, and as a result of the influence of, other voiced sounds. When the Roman alphabet was first used for writing English, as a rule either the difference between a voiced fricative and a voiceless one was not clear, or it was regarded as not important enough to distinguish in spelling, or it was taken as sufficiently suggested by the neighbouring letters. And in any event, it *was* sufficiently so indicated, so that separate letters for [v], [ð], and [z] were unnecessary: an understanding (certainly possessed by all literate Anglo-Saxons) of the 'rules' of OE word composition and pronunciation would show them unfailingly whether *f*, *þ* (*ð*), and *s* were to be taken as voiceless – [f], [θ], and [s] – or as voiced – [v], [ð], and [z]. Thus OE *ofer* was ['ɒvr], not ['ɒfr]; *ōþer* was ['ɪoːðr], not ['ɪoːθr]; and *risan* was ['riːzan], not ['riːsan]: all because the fricatives were both preceded and followed by voiced sounds.

ng. This digraph, at least when not final and possibly then too, usually represented [ŋg], not [ŋ] alone; i.e., the two sounds in NE *finger*, not the single one in *singer*. But when pre-historically followed by a high front vowel or semi-vowel, it apparently came to be fronted to [ndʒ], as in *sengan* ('singe'), ['sendʒan], *sengan* having been prehistorically ['saŋɣjan] and later ['seŋɣjan].

Double consonant letters indicated really double, or, more accurately, *long*, consonant sounds. E.g., OE *bucca* ('buck', 'he-goat') was ['buk:a] or ['buk-ka], not ['buka]: as in NE *book-case*, not as in *bookish*.

Simple Vowels

Long		Short	
ā: [aː]; as in *lacan*, 'to play'.		*a:* [a]; as in *macian*, 'to make'.	
ǣ: [æː]; as in *lǣdan*, 'to lead'.		*æ:* [æ]; as in *bæc*, 'back'.	
ē: [e]; as in *dēman*, 'to deem'.		*e:* [ɛ]; as in *helpan*, 'to help'.	
ī: [i]; as in *bītan*, 'to bite'.		*i:* [ɪ]; as in *scip*, 'ship'.	
ō: [o]; as in *bōtian*, 'to boot'.		*o:* [ɒ]; as in *ofte*, 'oft'.	
ū: [u]; as in *mūs*, 'mouse'.		*u:* [u]; as in *up(p)*, 'up'.	
ȳ: [y]; as in *mȳs*, 'mice'.		*y:* [ʏ]; as in *fyllan*, 'to fill'.	

Diphthongs
Long

ēa: (1) [æ:ə] or (2) [jæ:], depending at least originally on the etymology; e.g., (1) *bēam* ('tree'), [bæ:əm], earlier **baum* [baum]; (2) *cēace* ('cheek'), ['tʃjæ:kɛ], earlier **cæce* ['kæ:kɛ].

ēo: [eo] or [ɛo]; as in *flēogan*, 'to fly', ['ˈfleoɣɑn] or ['ˈflɛoɣɑn].

īe: [iə]; as in *hīeran*, 'to hear', ['ˈhiərɑn].

īo: [io] or [iə]; as in *līoht*, 'light' [lioxt] or [liəxt].

Short

ea: (1) [æə] or (2) [jæ], depending at least originally on the etymology; e.g., (1) *eald* ('old'), [æəld], earlier **æld* [æld]; (2) *sceal* ('shall'), [ʃjæl], earlier **scæl* [skæl].

eo: [ɛə]; as in *feoh*, 'money', 'property', [fɛəx].

ie: [ie]; as in *ieldra*, 'elder', ['ˈiəldra].

io: [io] or [iə]; as in *mioluc*, 'milk', ['ˈmioluk] or ['ˈmiəluk].

Having now seen what 'values' the letters of the alphabet had in OE, we may next properly enquire how they got these values. In general and to begin with, writers of OE naturally gave to the Roman letters the values usually attached to them in contemporary Latin. This was true even of *æ*, which in seventh-century Latin no longer, indeed, represented something like [æ:e], as it had in classical times, but on the other hand had not yet become confused (in Latin) with *e* [e] as it did later, but meant something very like [æ:]. It was accordingly the natural letter for the OE sound [æ:], and almost as natural for OE [æ], which was apprehended as the 'short' correlative of [æ:]. Again, *y* was the natural choice for [y] and [ʏ], for those were its values in contemporary Latin; it was not, there, a consonant. *Υ* is not a 'native' Latin letter, but a borrowing from Greek. In Latin, IE [u] and [ʊ] had generally remained unchanged, but in Greek they had generally been fronted to [y] and [ʏ]; and likewise, the corresponding Latin letter had taken the form *V*, whereas in Greek it was usually *Υ* (upsilon). When, in late antiquity, the Romans began worrying about the accurate transliteration of Greek words, they took to borrowing the Greek *Υ* (which they no longer identified with their own *V*) instead of contenting themselves, as they had earlier done, with transliterating it sometimes as *u* and sometimes as *i*. The adapters of the seventh-century Roman alphabet to the writing of English knew all this, and accordingly, when they came, in English, upon the sounds [y] and [Y] that they were familiar with in Greek loan-words, they naturally used the same symbol. The familiar modern English consonant use of *y* (for [j]) seems to have begun in the thirteenth century; for the very complex details, see the *New (Oxford) English Dictionary*, s.v. *Y*. The Greek origin of the letter, incidentally, is reflected in the French and German names, *i grec* and *ipsilon;* where the English name 'wye' [wɑi] comes from, no one knows.[1]

The letter *c* was adopted with the contemporary Latin value [k]; in later OE it gradually came in certain surroundings, as we have seen, to be pronounced [tʃ], but continued to be written. (Both these things, exactly, happened in Italian, but only by coincidence.) Somewhat, but not quite, the same thing happened to *g*, which in contemporary Latin represented [g], to which the closest approximation in the OE of the seventh century was [ɣ], for which the letter was accordingly utilized – and continued to be used for both [j] and [g] when those sounds developed, in certain surroundings, from [ɣ]. (In the latter case, then, *g* at length became, by accident, a more accurate symbol in OE than it had been to begin with.) The diphthongs are a special case. Some of the OE sounds written with two vowel letters were and (for the most part) always had been diphthongs, but most of them were originally monophthongs, and became diphthongs only after OE had begun to be written with Roman letters. E.g., most instances of *ea* and *eo* originated in the insertion of a 'glide' between a front vowel and a back consonant, *eald* [æəld] having been earlier [æld], and *feoh* [feəx] having been [fɛx]. These new sounds would ideally have been written respectively with *æ* or *e* plus some letter usually designating a non-front vowel – *a*, *o*, or *u*. But OE scribes recognised *æ* as formally *a* plus *e* (as indeed they sometimes wrote it), and, being prejudiced against writing three vowel letters in succession (as we still are), felt unwilling to follow *æ* or *ae* with any third vowel. Accordingly they took, quite arbitrarily, to representing [æ] when followed

[1] But see A. Campbell, *Old English Grammar* (Oxford 1959), p. 18, note 2.

C

by [ə] as *e*, and represented the [ə] by *a*. The question then arose of how they were to represent [ɛ] when followed by [ə]. They certainly realized that the second element of this diphthong, as of [æə], was a non-front vowel (though they didn't call it that, or, probably, anything – it must pretty certainly have been a concept without a name), and, indeed, the same non-front vowel as in [æə], but they could hardly use *ea* to represent [ɛə], since they had already used that for [æə]. This left them with two letters to choose from in order to represent the [ə] of [ɛə] – *o* and *u*. Since *u* was easily confused with *n* (in the usual handwriting of the time), and further, perhaps, since the sequence *eo* was familiar, and the sequence *eu* unknown, in other values, *o* was about all that was left, and it was accordingly adopted, so that [ɛə] came to be spelt *eo*. The exasperating result of all this was that the digraphs *ea* and *eo*, the same in the first part and different in the second, usually represent, in OE spelling, two diphthongs different in the first part and the same in the second.

The use of *ea* for [æə] raised some difficulties that were never completely met. (1) After the initial high front consonants [tʃ], [ʃ], and [j] (which were themselves for the most part late developments), a 'glide' developed between them and the following mid or low front vowels; to use an example already used, [skæl] became [ʃæl] and then [ʃjæl], the [j] being inserted as a transitional sound between the high front consonant [ʃ] and the low front vowel [æ]. It would perhaps have been more reasonable to write **sciæl* or even **scial*, but these sequences found little favour with the scribes, who preferred *sceal*, and preferred it without effective regard for the fact that *ea*, here used for [jæ], was already used, as we have seen, for [æə]. (2) It was bad enough to have *ea* representing two quite different sounds; it was, for some scribes, intolerable that it should represent also a third. As a consequence, *ea* representing the sound descended from Germanic [au] – probably [æːə] – was often distinguished by an acute accent, *éa* (replaced in most modern prints by a macron, *ēa*). But out of the frying pan: [æː], when preceded by certain high front fricatives, tended to develop a preceding glide, [j], just as [æ] did; and, the same objections obtaining to writing three successive vowel letters for the long sound as for the short, the only way of representing the new [jæ:] seemed to be *éa* (*ēa*). Thus, in the end, distinguishing the reflex of Germanic [au] from two other sounds by accenting the *e* did not serve to distinguish it from yet a fourth. In the light of all this, it is hardly surprising that OE scribes often omitted the acute accent in *ea* when that digraph stood for [æə] rather than for [æə] or [jæ]; for, even with the accent, it might stand for [jæ:] just as well as for [æ:ə]. And because of this frequent omission, the writers of modern editions and grammars are often obliged, in supplying or not supplying the *e* of an *ea* with a macron, to depend on inferences from etymology and from modern pronunciation; the practice in OE mss is wildly and hopelessly irregular. Some modern editions, in fact, omit macrons altogether, not only in *ea* but everywhere, and thus give, very possibly, a generally more satisfactory and in a way accurate impression of what OE mss are like or at least 'should' be like. In short, the OE scribal experiment with the acute accent and the nineteenth-century editorial experiment with the macron may almost be said to have been, on the whole, mistaken.

The spelling presented above is used with perfect consistency in hardly any extant mss – indeed, if we count acute accents (macrons in most modern texts), in none whatever. It is rather the way in which the most careful West Saxon scribes of the early part of the tenth century would have spelt if they had been perfectly consistent: it is normalized and even in a way idealized spelling. It is used in modern grammars not with any intention of concealing or denying the facts of OE usage, but in order to facilitate the student's learning the rudiments of the language. OE literary texts, as distinguished from illustrations in grammatical treatises, are nowadays always printed almost exactly letter for letter as they appear in the mss (except for the frequent systematic use of macrons).

Most extant OE mss, having been produced late in the tenth century or early in the eleventh, present a spelling even less 'normal' than the small number of mss of a century or so earlier. Thus (even quite early) we find final [x] after a vowel spelt sometimes *h*, sometimes *g*, probably because the sound was voiceless in some people's speech and voiced in others' – e.g., *genōh* and *genōg*, 'enough'. Again, for a variety of reasons, *ā* and *ǣ* were often interchanged – *āglǣca* and *ǣglǣca*, 'monster'; and

in LOE *æ* is often supplanted in some mss by *a*, in others by *e* –
probably a reflection of two divergent dialectal tendencies in
pronunciation, tendencies of which the first became dominant in
most dialects of EME. Yet again, *ī* is often supplanted by *ig*.
This comes about because *ig* at the end of a word stood for what
was historically [ij] or [ɪj], and, since it is almost impossible
to pronounce [j] except before a vowel, [ij] and [ɪj] at the
end of a word became practically identical with [i] – in, e.g.,
twentig, 'twenty', practically ['twɛnti]. OE scribes who made
little or no use of acute accents to distinguish long vowels were
not slow to adopt the digraph *ig* as a way of writing *i* [i], and
consequently wrote, e.g., *bigleofa*, 'sustenance', for what other
scribes, and all modern grammarians, would write *bīleofa*, in
accordance with the etymology; but *bigleofa* always meant [bi-],
never [bɪg-].

A somewhat similar case is illustrated by what is 'classically'
spelt *lufian*, 'to love', ['luvjɑn] or ['luviɑn] – the difference
between the consonantal high front [j] and the vocalic high
front [ɪ] is here practically negligible because of the absence of
stress on the sound concerned. Now the same or virtually the
same unstressed high front sound, vocalic or semi-vocalic,
developed, through absence of stress, in many other words
where the etymological spellings differed both from each other
and from that in *lufian*. Once the sounds shown by these several
spellings had become practically indistinguishable – had all
become some sort of unstressed high front sound, vocalic or
semi-vocalic, between other vowels – the spellings themselves
became, in large measure, practically interchangeable, with the
result that the classical West Saxon *lufian* appears in LOE documents not only as *lufian*, but also as *lufgian*, *lufgean*, *lufgan*,
lufigan, *lufegan*, *lufigean*, etc., etc. – all meant to represent
['luvjɑn] or ['luviɑn].

Two other confusions very common in LOE mss come from
the frequent use (1) of *y* (both short and long) for *ie* (both
short and long) – e.g., *bygan*, 'to bend' (and *bȳgean*, etc. – see
above) for *bīegan*, and (2) of *eo* (both short and long) for *io*
(both short and long) – e.g., *pēon*, 'to thrive', for *þion*. In the
first case, the probable cause was simply that the two pairs of
sounds originally indicated (in West Saxon) by *y* and *ie* became,

in the course of time, at least virtually identical; in the second that the two pairs of sounds originally indicated by *eo* and *io*, very similar to begin with, came to be shown increasingly by *eo* because that sequence of letters was for other reasons commoner and thus came to seem more natural. And yet some scribes prefer *io* for both sounds.

Yet two further kinds of irregular late spelling are rather different from those just discussed. In LOE, inflexional syllables – always final and always unstressed – began to be slurred, and hence similar ones began to be confused. Thus the EOE word-endings -*a*, -*e*, -*o* (sometimes), and -*u* all tended to assume, in LOE, the pronunciation [ə], and, correspondingly, late scribes are very uncertain and inconsistent about which of these letters they use in the unstressed final position. Likewise, *e* and *o* in the frequent terminations -*en* and -*on* both became [ə], and the final *m* of the very common termination -*um* tended to be shifted from the labial articulation to the dental or alveolar, [n], which in most phonetic situations takes less effort. Consequently, in the end, -*en* and -*on* came to be confused not only with each other but also with -*um*, and all three syllables came to be represented in LOE very commonly as -*on*, and in EME most commonly as -*en*.

Chapter VI

WHAT OLD ENGLISH MANUSCRIPTS
LOOK LIKE

★

W E M U S T begin this chapter, paradoxically, with 'what OE mss did *not* look like', or at least with 'what extant ones do not look like'. Specifically, they are written in the Roman alphabet, not some other. What the 'some other' might be expected to be is dealt with in the following paragraphs.

The Germanic invaders of Britain in the fifth and sixth centuries brought with them the alphabet or system of writing that they shared with all or almost all the Germanic peoples. These are the famous runes, or runic alphabet, or *futhark* (*futharc*, *futhork, futhorc*). Concerning the runes we must raise and try to answer two questions: (1) Why are they called runes (or what does *rune* mean)? (2) When and where and how did they originate?

(1) The word *rune* has cognates[1] in most of the Germanic languages. Its normal meaning is first 'whisper'[2] and then 'secret', 'mystery'; and it is anything but surprising that a barbarous and illiterate people should, almost superstitiously, apply such a name to what must have seemed to them the almost supernatural art of writing, which must have been as strange and impressive to them as, in succession, printing, the electric telegraph, the telephone, the radio, and television have been – or would have been but for the wearying and dulling of the sense of wonder – to their descendants. S. F. B. Morse's first message by the electric telegraph was 'What hath God wrought?'; the

[1] Cognates – words (in 'ancestrally' related languages) springing from a common original word in the 'ancestral' language; e.g., Italian and Spanish *padre* and French *père* are cognates, having their common origin in Latin *patrem*, which in turn is cognate with English *father* (OE *fæder*), with which it shares a common IE 'ancestor'.

[2] The related OE verb *rūnian*, 'whisper', preserved in the (archaic) NE 'round one in the ear', reflects the earliest sense.

70

same feeling some two thousand years earlier prompted the
Germanic barbarians to call writing a mystery.

(2) As for the origin of the runes, there is no doubt that they
are modifications of what we can call the Greek alphabet if we
include, as we should, the Roman alphabet as a variety of the
Greek, and that they came into being at least as early as A.D. 200.
The ancient Teutons apparently became acquainted with this
alphabet chiefly through inscriptions on Greek or Roman coins
and other artifacts that occasionally found their way north. The
runes owe some, at least, of their differences from contemporary
Greek and Roman letters to the modifications more or less
automatically induced by the writing surface, which seems to
have been originally slips of wood or bark (especially beech),[1]
and by the writing tool, a knife: the runes avoid both curves
and horizontal lines. Most extant runic inscriptions are on stone,
and were produced with chisel and mallet, and these materials
and instruments do not, at least to the same degree, give rise
to the same practical limitations of letter form; but (1) the
forms dictated by the original wood and knife were naturally
imitated, on stone and by chisel and mallet, and (2) stone is
almost infinitely more durable than wood. When incised wood or
chiselled stone came to be imitated on vellum or other parchment
inscribed with an ink-filled reed or pen, the letters not unnatur-
ally retained much of the original rectilinear and angular form.

We do not know by what fraction of this or that ancient
Germanic tribe the runes were understood or used, nor do
we know to what extent they were used for correspondence,
chronicles, or literature. The vast majority of runic texts now
extant (the earliest are Scandinavian,[2] and of the third century)
are lapidary and for the most part what may be called inscrip-

---

[1] *Beech* is from OE *bēce* [ˈbetʃɛ], which is radically identical with OE *bōc*
[bok], whence NE *book*. The phonetic relation between *beech* and *book* (which
is perfectly regular), and the sematic also, is further illuminated by the
fact that the OE nominative and accusative plural of *bōc* was *bēc* [betʃ],
which would have yielded **beech* in NE.

[2] This is reflected in the form of the NE word *rune*. It is first recorded
in 1690 (according to the *New* (or *Oxford*) *English Dictionary*), and is not
descended from the OE form but borrowed from the ON, which had remained
in use with approximately the original common Germanic pronunciation,

tional – dedicative, memorial, funerary, and monumental. It is almost as if we had little ancient Roman writing but what we get from such monuments as Trajan's Column or the tombs in the Roman catacombs.

The earliest extant document in OE is of, apparently, the year 679, by which time runes had ceased to be used (if they had ever been used) for everyday writing (if there was any everyday writing) and had given way to the Roman alphabet for all ordinary purposes. A few extant OE mss contain runes, but only incidentally and in secondary and for the most part nugatory functions – in quasi-acrostics, in riddles and semi-riddles, in mnemonic verses, and the like. (A fairly close parallel can be found in the occasional use today, say on Christmas cards and in certain legal forms, of black-letter or 'Old English' type.)

The commonest variety of the runic alphabet had twenty-four letters (to which some half-dozen were occasionally added in English use), usually conceived and memorized in an order completely different from and unrelated to that of the Greek and Roman alphabets (*a*, *b*, etc.). For the last century or so it has been more or less customary to call this runic alphabet the *futhark* (*futharc, futhork, futhorc*), from the sounds designated by the first six runes, the equivalents (in OE) of *f* [f, v], *u* [u, ʊ], *th* [θ, ð], *æ*[1] [æ:, æ], *r* [r], *k* (or *c*) [k, tʃ].

The runes do not seem to have been commonly called, however, by the names of the sounds they designated, but by words (nouns) beginning with those sounds: thus the *f*-rune was called

whereas the OE word, if it had not gone out of use, would theoretically (and probably) have become NE **rown* [raun] – or, with excrescent *d* as in the related verb, **round*.

[1] Why not, then, 'futhærk', etc., rather than 'futhark', etc.? Because the rune for OE [æ] had been in Primitive Germanic the rune for [ɑ], of which [æ] is the commonest OE reflex, and the name *futhark* was bestowed rather from a general (Primitive Germanic) point of view than from a specific (OE) one. For the comparatively few cases in which the OE reflex of Primitive Germanic [ɑ] is [ɑ] instead of [æ], Anglo-Saxon users of the runes developed a modified form of the original *a*-rune, but the original one retained its place in the conventional order. The forms *futhork*, *futhorc* are explained in a somewhat similar way: Primitive Germanic *a* became in certain circumstances *o* in ON.

feoh ('cattle', 'property', 'money'), the *th*-rune *þorn* ('thorn'),
the *w*-rune *wynn* ('joy'), one of the *e*-runes *ēþel* ('homeland'),
etc. It is this habit of calling the runes by such names that makes
possible their 'shorthand' use. One notable instance of this is
the occasional substitution of the *ēþel*-rune (an *X* with an inverted
V surmounting it and thus forming a 'diamond' with the top of
the *X*) for the word *ēþel* (earlier *ǣþel*) spelt out, in several
extant OE mss (notably that of *Beowulf*). Yet more remarkable
are the 'runic signatures' of Cyn(e)wulf, a poet of the eighth
century or early ninth, who has left two poems in the 'Exeter
Book' and two in the 'Vercelli' (both mss dating from the early
part of the eleventh century, and hence certainly not Cynewulf's
autographs[1] – removed from them, indeed, in all probability, by
several stages). These poems he has 'signed' by so contriving
his verses that the seven (or eight) runes spelling his name (a)
occur in the order of the letters of his name, and (b) make
sense in the context when taken as 'shorthand'. E.g., the rune
called *wynn* (meaning 'joy' and formed like a *P* with a wedge-
shaped 'loop') is so placed that it does double duty: (1) as
equivalent to *w* in the quasi-acrostic spelling of the poet's name,
and (2) as the shorthand of the word *wynn*. Scarcely any more
ingenious and fool-proof method has ever been hit upon of
perpetuating an author's name; and the method worked quite
literally unique success for Cynewulf, who is the only certainly
surviving OE poet – the only certainly surviving substantially
productive one, at least – whose name we certainly know. This
denomination of letters by words beginning with the designated
sound is, incidentally, closely parallel with the practice of the
ancient Phoenician or other Semitic inventors or disseminators
of the alphabet of which the Greek and Roman are varieties.
The Hebrew names, e.g., of the first three letters – *aleph*, *beth*,
gimel – mean respectively 'ox', 'house', and 'camel', and these
were taken over, along with the letters, mechanically from
Semitic by Greek in the forms *alpha*, *beta*, *gamma*, which are
quite meaningless in Greek. The Romans and their European
pupils, on the other hand, said simply *a* [ɑ:], *b* [be], *c* [ke], etc.

[1] We shall do well to remind ourselves here that the modern colloquial
restriction of the word *autograph* to the meaning 'the *name* of a (usually
well-known) person written by his own hand' *is* modern and colloquial.

The Anglo-Saxons, despite their knowledge of the runes, can hardly be said to have been in any very important or decided way a literate people much before St Augustine's Roman mission of 597. St Augustine and his companions brought with them the Italian alphabet and handwriting of their day, and used it, certainly, in composing and copying Latin. They probably also used it to some extent in the more or less experimental writing of English, but of such experiments there are hardly any vestiges, and the extant OE mss (a few from as early as shortly before 700, but most of them from the tenth and eleventh centuries) are almost all written not in an Italian hand, but in a variety of the hand developed in Ireland in the sixth and seventh centuries and conveyed to the Anglo-Saxons through Irish monasteries in northern England. (A modern printed adaptation of this is used in Ireland in our own day for Irish, and may be seen, e.g., on Irish coins.) This was originally and essentially identical with Continental hands (and with the many handwritten and printed forms of the Roman alphabet familiar to us), but, like all styles of writing (and printing), had certain peculiarities.

In this hand, the following letters anyone can usually recognize at once and with ease, through their close resemblance to one or another of the forms familiar to us: *a, b, c, e, h, k, l, m, n, o, p, q, u, x, y,* and *z*. The letters *k, q,* and *z* were seldom used; and *j, v,* and *w* are more or less recent inventions, or rather their specialization as letters distinct from *i, u,* and *uu* (*vu, vv*) is more or less recent.[1] This leaves, as puzzles for the beginner, *d, f, g, i, r, s,* and *t*. Though fashions differed from time to time,

---

[1] The modern forms *v* and *j* develop from secondary forms of *u* and *i* used quite early here and there, but originally as accidental and then ornamental variations. The form *u* is the normal semicursive development of *V* elsewhere than initially; initially, there was a tendency, followed by some but not all writers, to start the first stroke higher and end it lower, and to form it with both a beginning and an ending flourish, with the result that it tended to meet the second stroke at an angle. (The modern *v*, then, despite its appearance at least in roman type, is in the main not immediately derived from *V*, but is originally an automatic variation of *u*.) Hence the form *v* normally appeared, when it appeared at all, only as the first letter of a word. Now it happens (1) that in Latin an initial *u* (or *v*) is consonantal – [v], earlier [w] – between three and four times oftener than it is

from district to district, and from individual to individual, we may describe the usual forms of these letters in most extant OE mss as follows: *d* – made in a single curvilinear stroke – an *o* beginning at the top, proceeding counterclockwise, and shooting off spirally toward the upper left on the completion of the circle. *f* – 'F', but with the lower cross bar on the writing line, and the 'tail' below it. *g* – made sometimes very like the figure 3, sometimes more like the figure 5, with the 'tails' below the line. *i* – usually undotted. *r* – like 'p', but with the loop deflected, at the bottom, to the right, instead of being brought round to the upright again. *s* – made in three ways: like 'f', but with little or no cross bar; in the same way, but with the cross bar (or the place where the cross bar would be) on the line, and the tail extending below it; like 'r' with the upright stroke lengthened downwards and descending below the line. *t* – like 'c' with a horizontal stroke on top of it. *y*, also, sometimes looks a little strange because it is often dotted (between the 'horns') – especially, oddly enough, when *i* is not. For these letters, ordinary modern types are commonly substituted today. Besides these letters, OE also, as we have seen, took over from

vocalic, [u] or [ʊ], and (2) that a non-initial *u* is much more often vocalic: the chances were, i.e., than an initial *u* was [v], and a medial or final one [u] or [ʊ]. From this it was no great step to writing (or rather printing) *v* for the consonant and *u* for the vowel not only initially but everywhere. The specialization of the form *j* as consonantal is often said to have come about in exactly the same way, but this can hardly be true, for (1) that form originally occurs as a substitute for *i*, when it occurs at all, oftener at the end of a word than at the beginning, and (2) *i* or *j* is consonantal much less often than it is vocalic, not only medially and finally, but also initially. The consonantal specialization of *j*, then, apparently must be explained rather altogether as a comparatively arbitrary choice of the less usual form for the less usual value, whereas this motive operated only secondarily in the consonantal specialization of *v*. Until well within the eighteenth century, alphabetical indexes and the like, though they distinguish *i* and *j*, *u* and *v* functionally in the modern fashion, commonly treated them as identical for alphabetizing purposes; e.g., the alphabetical order of *in*, *joy*, *ire* was that rather than *in*, *ire*, *joy*. The modern form *w* comes not so much from the occasional OE *vu* or *uu* or *vv* as from a later French interlacing of the two *v*'s, occurring normally only at the beginning of a word.

contemporary Latin use a ligature, *æ* (*a* plus *e*, and sometimes written that way), which virtually counted as a separate letter. (A degenerate form of *æ* – *e* with a hook like a reversed comma under it – is found in some mss.) This letter (*æ*) is nowadays conveniently called (in speaking of its OE use) 'ash', the name (in the OE form *æsc*) of the corresponding rune (corresponding, i.e., in name and 'value', not in form, which was like 'F' with the cross bars slanting downwards instead of being horizontal).

For a time this Latin alphabet, unmodified, was used by the Anglo-Saxons in writing their own language. But that language contained three sounds that this alphabet could not unambiguously express – $[\theta]$, $[\eth]$, and $[w]$. For a while, $[\theta]$ and $[\eth]$ were written *th* (as they have come to be again since the fourteenth century), and $[w]$ was written *u* or *uu* (or *v*, *vu*, *vv*). But these were not satisfactory expedients. The digraph *th* was adopted by the Romans, when they began to be fussy about the accurate transliteration of Greek words containing θ (theta), pronounced $[\theta]$ in Greek at least since the early Christian centuries, and hence familiar in that value to learned men in Western Europe in those centuries and even later. (In the seventh and eighth centuries, in England especially, there were many good Greek scholars – far more than in the later middle ages.) But θ, in such Greek words having it as entered (through Latin) into the vernaculars of Western Europe, was pronounced $[t]$ by the relatively unlearned, to whom therefore *th* suggested rather $[th]$ or even merely $[t]$ (hardly distinguishable from $[th]$), and it was accordingly always in danger of seeming to be merely a complex and pretentious way of writing *t*. Writers of OE consequently cast about for a less ambiguous symbol – and found two of them. One was a mere modified *d* – $\eth$, the symbol adopted, in the phonetic alphabet used in this book, for the voiced dental spirant (as in *then*). It is called 'crossed *d*' and sometimes, by modern scholars, 'eth' or 'edh' $[\varepsilon\eth]$. The other was a rune, *þ* (thorn). Oddly and annoyingly enough, from a modern point of view, eth and thorn were *both* used for *both* voiceless $[\theta]$ and voiced $[\eth]$. Some mss mix them without apparent system; some use this or that according to the ease with which the pen could proceed from the last letter or to the next (somewhat as many people today use two kinds of *e* or *r* or *s* or *t*); others use thorn initially and eth elsewhere; others use one or the other exclusively. As we have seen, this made no real difficulty for the Anglo-Saxon reader, and seldom need make any for us, but it does seem a little odd, to our orderly and systematic minds, that, so long as both letters were adopted, they were not assigned separate phonetic significations.

One other rune was adopted in the writing of OE, viz. *wynn* (the name means 'joy'; the usual form was much like that of thorn without the ascending vertical stroke, and was often confusingly like that of *p*). Its value was [w], and nowadays *w* is usually substituted for it in printing OE, though *æ*, *þ*, and *ð* are all kept. In Latin, consonant *u* (as in *uictor*, 'victor') had originally designated [w] but had come considerably before the seventh century to designate [v]; and *u* (or *v*) was consequently no longer a clear way of writing [w], which was a common sound in OE. So was [v]; we have already seen why *v* (or *u*) was not ordinarily and did not need to be used for this sound, as well as why *f* could be and ordinarily was.

From *c.* A.D. 1000, French letter forms begin to appear in English mss, at first only in French and Latin words and passages, but later in English ones as well; by *c.* 1150, most English handwriting had become virtually identical with French except that thorn continued in use (French having no unambiguous symbol for the sounds it designated) as did the native *g* alongside the French one. Eth disappeared, and *w* (or *vu*, etc.) was substituted for wynn.

A number of abbreviations were in common use, most of them, naturally enough, more or less imitations of contemporary Latin usage. Thus what is in form a macron (ˉ) or a tilde (˜) over a vowel stands for a following *m*, especially in the almost universal dative plural ending of nouns and adjectives, *-um*, and, over the *n* in *poⁿ*, for the *-ne* of *ponne* ('then'). The same sign is sometimes used over an initial *g* to stand for the *e* of the very common initial syllable *ge*. About equally common is an ampersand[1] almost exactly like the figure '7', used as shorthand

---

[1] Ampersand. This name is perhaps properly (and was at any rate originally) bestowed only on '&', which is merely (in form) a degenerate 'et' (Latin for 'and'), but it is usefully applied also to any single sign, in

not only for the independent conjunction *and* or *ond* but also for the same sequence of letters occurring (as they often do) as the (usually initial) element of a compound word. It is very ancient in origin (going all the way back to 'Tironian Notes', the system of shorthand ascribed to Cicero's favourite secretary Tiro), and results from joining a macron or a tilde with the down-stroke of a following 'T'. Very frequently a thorn with a horizontal stroke across the ascending vertical means *þæt*, and sometimes the same sign plus *te* means *þætte*.

Capital letters were, according to our standards, used rarely, sporadically, and unsystematically. There are two kinds of capital letters – large and conspicuous and ornamental ones, usually found singly, and smaller ones, usually found in sequences of anywhere from a syllable to a whole line. Both are most commonly used to distinguish the beginnings of more or less independent constituents of a ms text, the large, single, and strictly ornamental kind being usually left by the scribe to an illuminator (who sometimes never got round to doing his job, and consequently left a gap in the ms), and the smaller kind (most commonly in sequences) being usually written by the scribe himself, who sometimes differentiated them very slightly from the ordinary text except by size.

The case of what looks like a capital *I* is rather special. A long or otherwise distinctive form of *i* is useful in many hands because, without some distinction, it is often easily overlooked in cursive or semi-cursive hands, or confused with one of the upright strokes of *u*, *n*, or *m* (though this possibility occurs rather oftener in ME than in OE hands). One way of making it clear that a vertical stroke is the independent letter *i* is to lengthen it; another is to surmount it with a dot or an acute accent. The former method survives, more or less, in our *I* and *J*, the latter in our *i*, and both together in our *j*. A good many OE mss lengthen the *i* instead of accenting (or dotting) it, and accordingly a good many show what looks like a capital *I* very generally – not only (though sometimes especially) as as initial. The forms *I* and *i*, and later *j* (and still later *J*) are, in other words, merely, in the writing any language, for the word meaning 'and' in that language. *Ampersand* is 'and per se and'; the Scottish equivalent, *epershand*, is similarly 'et per se and'.

main, various ways of making it plain that a down-stroke is to be taken by itself rather than as a constituent of another letter commonly made with two or three identical down-strokes.

Long and short vowels, usually distinguished nowadays, in printing OE, by a macron over the long ones, are, in many OE mss, left without any distinction. When they are marked, the usual mark is an acute accent, not a macron; and the marking in most mss is sporadic, inconsistent, and often demonstrably inaccurate, and sometimes little short of whimsical – so whimsical that we are actually driven to conclude that some copyists regarded the marks as mere decorations. The fact probably is that many extant mss owe their length-marks to what we might call editors of the exemplars,[1] who, according to their taste and fancy, inserted marks of the general character of acute accents to distinguish sometimes long vowels, sometimes alliterated or other stressed syllables, sometimes syllables calling for either logical or rhetorical emphasis or both, and sometimes, finally, merely words in some way or other remarkable in the eyes of this or that reader through whose hands the ms had passed. It is no wonder that copyists sometimes came to imagine that acute accents were decorations, to be sprinkled and let fall alike upon the just and the unjust.

In some mss the beginnings of sections are indicated by preceding blank lines, either along with or instead of capital letters. Spacing between sentences is seldom uniformly greater than between words, and spacing between words is often not uniformly greater than spacing between the elements of a compound word. Verse is most commonly written as prose (for economy's sake); where a metrical line begins and ends can be made out only from a knowledge of the laws of OE metrics.

Punctuation is rare, sporadic, and above all (from a modern point of view) inconsistent and unsystematic and often virtually meaningless. Some mss have almost no punctuation; those that have, we might often wish followed the same practice. Most of those that use punctuation with some degree of what appeals to the modern mind as reason use several marks – a raised or 'centred' period, a colon, a semicolon (but neither of them with

[1] Exemplar – the ms copied from by a scribe (or by a printer) in producing another ms (or printed text).

anything like their fairly precise modern values), a colon plus the OE 'ampersand' (see above), a colon plus a centred tilde, a period surmounted by a check-mark – more or less as marks sometimes of prosodical and sometimes (less often) of rhetorical division. Some mss assemble a number of repeated 'points' to mark the end of a section, much in the manner of the grouped asterisks and the like of modern printers (who derived such practices from similar ones in mss); the practice has about the same purpose and utility as the modern newspaper reporter's conclusion of his 'copy' with '30', meaning conventionally 'finis'.

One use of punctuation (in the strict and general sense of adding 'points' – dots and the like – to a text) that occurs rather often in OE mss is a device for indicating desired omission of letters and words written by mistake, viz., a dot beneath each letter to be omitted – a neater and more sightly method than 'crossing out'. This use of subscript dots is reasonably enough called 'expunction' (a 'pointing *out of* [the text]'), and the ordinary modern use of *expunge* in the sense 'delete' derives from it.

Extant OE mss are seldom written in a cursive (or 'running') hand; the letters, i.e., are seldom connected, as in most modern handwriting, but separate, as in modern printing. They are usually also upright (like roman type) rather than slanted to the right (like italic). Such variations in handwriting come about partly from the writing materials (stone, wood, wax tablets, parchment, papyrus, paper; chisel, knife, stylus, brush, reed, quill, metal pen), partly from the angle at which the pen (or other writing instrument) is held; partly, in the case of pens, from the width of the nib and the angle at which it is cut; partly, according to this traditional convention or that, from the nature of the text (poetry, homily, missal, chronicle, charter); partly from the language (Latin, English, French); partly from consideration of the reader for whose use the ms is intended (oneself, fellow members of a monastery, lay patron, minstrel), partly from the status of the copyist (professional, semi-professional, amateur): but most of all from the slow and largely unconscious evolution of fashion or style, of which the laws are past finding out. The general tendency, in the development of handwriting, is for the writer's ease to be preferred to the reader's until in the course of time a reform, for the reader's benefit, becomes practically imperative. Extant OE mss, generally speaking, are a good deal easier for us to read (apart from a few peculiar Celtic and runic forms) than ME, and are so mainly because in the tenth and eleventh centuries (at least in England) the reader happened to be ahead, and, in the fourteenth and fifteenth, the writer. We must also remember that almost all extant OE mss were executed with the degree of care befitting a record meant to be comparatively permanent and comparatively public: they corresponded, i.e., rather to the modern printed book than to the modern handwritten private diary or letter. We know next to nothing about the hands in which the Anglo-Saxons wrote designedly private and ephemeral documents.

Chapter VII

OLD ENGLISH WORDS AND WORD FORMS

★

W H E N we examined the OE version of *St Luke* ii some chapters earlier, we observed illustrations of a number of striking differences between OE and ME. Two of these we may well take up here in a little more detail, since the passage from the Gospel hardly exemplifies them sufficiently, viz., inflexion and vocabulary.

NE inflects exceptionally few words and inflects them in an exceptionally small number of ways. OE differs in both these respects: it is a little more variously if not more frequently inflected than modern German, and hardly less frequently – and in some ways more variously – than Latin. This is not true, to be sure, of verbs, which are almost as simple in OE as they are, fundamentally,[1] in NE and German, and much simpler than in

---

[1] 'Fundamentally' is an important qualification, if we restrict, as we may do, the term 'inflexion' to *changes in* (most often the endings of) *single words* and exclude distinctions that consist in the *piling up of several* words. Thus in Latin, the single word *vidi* expresses what NE needs three words to express, 'I have seen'; and similarly Latin *videbo* equals NE 'I shall see', and Latin *videbar* equals NE 'I was being seen'. The resources of OE (and of most other early Germanic languages) for expressing such differences in tense and voice were, compared with Latin, very slender: they did not include, primitively, any generally used and accepted way of differentiating the perfect ('I have seen') or the 'progressive' past ('I was seeing') from the simple past ('I saw'); or, more surprisingly, the future ('I shall see') from the present. OE commonly left these distinctions to be gathered from the context, or, for the passive ('it is seen'), substituted the equivalent of 'one sees'. (Note that we still sometimes express the future by means of the present: 'The train leaves at 7 a.m. tomorrow.' And for 'one sees' instead of 'it is seen', cf. French '*on voit*' – which itself imitates a Germanic idiom.) LOE made a start towards the use of the verbs 'have', 'be', 'shall', 'will', and others in forming, with the infinitives and past participles of other verbs, phrasal equivalents of what Latin usually expresses by changes in single words. These phrasal equivalents are called 'periphrastic' (i.e.,

Latin; but OE nouns and adjectives were very elaborately (and very variously) inflected indeed. In the first place, OE nouns (like Latin and German ones, and unlike NE) had grammatical *gender* – i.e., were regarded as what is technically called masculine, feminine, or neuter – and the demonstratives (or articles) and adjectives modifying a noun varied their forms according to the gender of the noun. Thus 'the old tree' is *sē ealda bēam* (masculine), 'the old birch-tree' is *sēo ealde beorc* (feminine), and 'the old leaf' is *þæt ealde lēaf* (neuter). Every OE noun has gender; and to make matters worse (1) what the gender is is usually, as in the examples, not determinable from the nominative singular form, and (2) gender has little fixed or dependable relation to sex; the names of at least as many inanimate (i.e., conventionally or actually sexless) objects are masculine or feminine as are neuter, and, oddly enough, the names of some animate beings – even human beings – are neuter: e.g., *wīf* ('woman', 'wife') and *cild* ('child').[1]

This situation will hardly surprise or dismay a student of Latin or French, but the same cannot be said of the existence in

'circumlocutory', 'roundabout'). The striking difference, in this respect, between OE and NE is that even LOE used such periphrases only sporadically and inconsistently and, one might almost say, carelessly and uncomprehendingly and wastefully, whereas NE has refined them into an extraordinarily rich and subtle and rigorous system – at least the equivalent, in expressiveness and definiteness, of the Latin system. And yet there remains a fundamental way in which the difference between, e.g., *vidi* ('I have seen') and *videbam* ('I was seeing'), or between *video* ('I see) and *videor* ('I am seen'), is a difference in *inflexion* in a sense in which the difference between the NE equivalents is not. In short, Latin did a great deal by means of inflexion (in the narrow and primary sense); EOE did much less, but by essentially the same means; LOE did rather more than EOE, but less than Latin or NE, and less regularly and clearly and systematically – and did it by means of periphrases rather than of inflexion proper; NE does even more than Latin did, and does it by extending and systematizing the use and meaning of the periphrases.

[1] The origins of grammatical gender in the IE languages (in which it is primitively pervasive) are obscure and disputed; though the distinction is more or less involved with sex in the recorded languages, even the earliest ones, that association is probably accidental and of comparatively late origin.

OE (and in at least the early stages of all the other Germanic languages) of two complete and distinct ways of inflecting almost all adjectives: in some situations (most notably when the definite article precedes the adjective), the so-called 'weak declension'[1] of the adjective is used, and in others (most notably when the adjective is in the predicate, after the verb 'to be'), the so-called 'strong declension'. The number of the declensions of nouns, also, is a good deal greater than in Latin – OE has ten each in the masculine and feminine, and nine in the neuter. Some of these, however, include far more nouns than others; and below are printed the declensions of the three specimens given above, each of which belongs to the commonest declension of its gender. Before each form in these declensions of nouns are printed the appropriate forms of the definite article (or demonstrative pronoun – it means both 'the' and 'that') and of the weak declension of the adjective; and after each, the appropriate 'strong' form. There is in practice a certain amount of variation from dialect to dialect, from period to period, and even within a single dialect or period: the following tables present only the commonest and most nearly 'classical' or 'standard' West Saxon forms.

	Article	Weak adjective	Noun	Strong adjective
Masculine, *bēam*, 'tree'				
Singular				
Nominative	sē	ealda	bēam	eald
Accusative	þone	ealdan	bēam	ealdne
Genitive	þæs	ealdan	bēames	ealdes
Dative	þǣm	ealdan	bēame	ealdum
Instrumental	þȳ	ealdan	bēame	ealde
Plural				
Nom., Acc.	þā	ealdan	bēamas	ealde
Genitive	þāra	ealdena	bēama	ealdra
Dat., Instr.	þǣm	ealdum	bēamum	ealdum

[1] Declension – the set of forms (of an adjective or noun or pronoun) varying with the case and number.

	Article	Weak adjective	Noun	Strong adjective

Feminine, *beorc*, 'birch-tree'

Singular

	Article	Weak adjective	Noun	Strong adjective
Nominative	sēo	ealde	beorc	eald
Accusative	þā	ealdan	beorce	ealde
Gen., Dat., Instr.	þære	ealdan	beorce	ealdre

Plural

Nom., Acc.	þā	ealdan	beorca	ealda
Genitive	þāra	ealdena	beorca	ealdra
Dat., Instr.	þæm	ealdum	beorcum	ealdum

Neuter, *lēaf*, 'leaf'

Singular

Nom., Acc.	þæt	ealde	lēaf	eald
Genitive	þæs	ealdan	lēafes	ealdes
Dative	þæm	ealdan	lēafe	ealdum
Instrumental	þȳ	ealdan	lēafe	ealde

Plural

Nom., Acc.	þā	ealdan	lēaf	eald
Genitive	þāra	ealdena	lēafa	ealdra
Dat., Instr.	þæm	ealdum	lēafum	ealdum

Another particular of inflexion in which OE differs conspicuously from NE is in the number of 'strong' verbs. Almost all verbs in English (and in other Germanic languages) of every period can be classified as either 'strong' or 'weak'. A weak verb forms its preterite and its past participle by adding to the basic element of the present-tense form a syllable or syllables containing a 'dental' (actually nowadays in English alveolar, but still always called, in this connexion, dental) sound: e.g., (NE) *greet* (present), *greeted* (preterite and past participle) (and, much less obviously but just as truly, in origin, *beseech-besought* and *set-set*). How *besought* and *set* (preterite and past participle) can be said to have originated merely by adding to (early forms of) *beseech* and *set* (present) a syllable or syllables containing a dental sound is worth looking into, partly to assuage the reader's natural incredulity, but partly also to illustrate the principle that sound changes proceed by degrees – that a NE sound did not suddenly replace a very different ME or OE sound but is rather the latest stage in a series of changes from one sound to another differing only slightly from it both in auditory effect and in physiological mode of production.

Let us take *beseech-besought* first. In prehistoric OE, the infinitive (representing the present) must have been approximately [bɪˈsokjɑn] and the preterite and past participle basically [bɪˈsoxt-]. (It would take a disproportionately long time and carry us unreasonably far back into IE to explain why [x] appears in the second form instead of [k]; but note that the difference is of exactly the kind that we are considering here, viz., a very slight one, [k] being the voiceless velar, or palatal, stop and [x] the voiceless velar, or palatal, fricative.) As a rule, speakers of any language tend, through instinctive laziness, to change the position and operation of the vocal organs as little as possible between consecutive sounds; and this means, in effect, that the articulation of one sound tends to approximate to itself the articulation of a neighbouring sound and thus, in the end, to alter the neighbouring sound. In [bɪˈsokjɑn], [k] was at first a velar sound, because the preceding [o] was so. But the following [j] was produced by contact between tongue and palate at a much more forward part of the mouth; and gradually, to ease the transition from front to back, [k] was articulated further and further forward in the mouth till, at length, conjoined, so to speak, with the following [j], it ceased to be a [k] at all and became the affricate [tʃ]. The result of this process alone would have been [bɪˈsotʃɑn]. But this process did not occur alone; a chain reaction was going on at the same time. The back [k], while in the process of being fronted by and more or less coalescing with the following front [j], itself in turn tended to front the preceding back vowel [o], which accordingly first became [ɸ] (mid back round to mid front round) and then [e] (mid front round to mid front unround, through the tendency, common in English and in most languages, for round front vowels eventually to lose their roundness, which is in a sense an unnatural combination with frontness); and thus [bɪˈsotʃɑn] became first [bɪˈsɸtʃan] and then [bɪˈsetʃan]. Finally, in ENE, [e] was regularly raised to [i], and (we may ignore here the disappearance of the third syllable) the result was NE [bɪˈsitʃ], 'beseech'. The development of the preterite and past participle (basically [bɪˈsoxt-]) was quite divergent, but proceeded just as gradually, unconsciously, and 'naturally'. The [o] here is, as we have seen, a mid back sound; the following [x] is high back. After the [x] there was no high front sound as there was after the [k] in the present. Since [x] accordingly did not tend to become fronted, it did not itself tend to front the preceding [o]. But [x], though like [o] in being back, is unlike it in being high rather than mid, and, in EME, influenced the [o] to the extent of adding to it a high back vowel by way of transition from mid back vowel to high back consonant; i.e., the monophthong [o] became the diphthong [ou]. When a monophthong becomes a diphthong by adding a second vowel to the original one, both (especially the first) tend to become shorter, and short vowels, as we have seen, tend to be lower than the corresponding long vowels; consequently in LME [ou] became [ɒu] (mid back round to low back round). Meanwhile, Southern English generally was developing and extending a tendency to get rid (why, heaven knows) of the sound [x], which survives only in Northern NE, especially Scots, though our spelling, which generally reflects early fifteenth-century pronunciation, retains, in 'besought', the 'gh' which was the usual ME spelling of [x] (in OE the usual spelling was simply 'h', as we have seen). The disappearance of this high back consonant had two effects: (1) the [u], so to speak, was deprived of its reason for existence, and accordingly disappeared; (2) the remaining [ɒ] was 'compensatorily' lengthened to [ɔ], leaving NE [bɪˈsɔt]. [bɪˈsɔt] is a long way from [bɪˈsoxt-], but the word has travelled that long way by short stages; and *besought* proves (disregarding, as before, the extremely early presence of [x] in the preterite instead of the [k] of the present) to have been originally just as essentially and fundamentally present plus dental as *greeted* from *greet* is.

Set-set is a much simpler case and a somewhat different one. The OE infinitive (representing the present) was *settan*. The preterite was *sette* (*set-* plus *-te*), and the past participle, *set(t)*.

In LME, such inflexional final syllables as those of *settan* and *sette* ceased to be pronounced, and, later, spelt, with the result that the present, preterite, and past participle have all become identical – 'set'. The fact remains, however, that *set* is a weak verb, which originally formed its preterite and past participle by adding a dental sound to the present. The disappearance of this added dental as a distinct entity is owing to the accident that the basic present form *set*- itself ended in a dental, with which the added dental of the preterite and the past participle coalesced. Therefore, though *beseech-besought* and *set-set* may be called 'irregular' verbs (as compared with the 'regular' *greet-greeted*), they are historically classifiable with it as weak rather than with *sing-sang-sung* or *write-wrote-written* as strong.

A weak verb, then, is one that inherits its now-existing secondary forms (preterite and past participle) from forms originating in the addition of a dental sound to the (basic form of the) present. A strong verb, on the other hand, generates its secondary forms by altering the vowel and (more importantly) does *not* add a dental sound: e.g., NE *sing-sang-sung* or *write-wrote-written*. OE had about three hundred strong verbs, of which a little fewer than a quarter survive at least in part as strong verbs; roughly a half have disappeared from use; and the rest (a little more than a quarter) have become weak. (E.g., OE *rīdan-rād-riden* survives in NE as a strong verb – *ride, rode, ridden*; whereas OE *glīdan-glād-gliden*, which would theoretically and analogically have yielded NE *glide-*glode-*glidden*, has become weak – *glide-glided*.

The OE version of *St Luke* ii, then, insufficiently illustrates the degree to which OE was more elaborately or variously inflected than NE. It illustrates still more insufficiently the ways in which OE differed from NE in vocabulary; not because the vocabulary of the NE version is much larger, for it is not so, and is not so, naturally enough, because every one of the four versions speaks of the same simple (however momentous) things and speaks of them simply. The trouble is that the average reader of this book, who is perhaps not likely to have seen or at any rate examined any other piece of OE, is, on the other hand, well aware of how very extensive the NE vocabulary is; and in consequence he is likely to make an unconscious comparison of the vocabulary of this particular OE passage with the whole vocabulary of the NE he knows rather than with the vocabulary of the NE version of the passage, and ends with the impression that the total vocabulary of OE was much smaller than it actually was.

In speaking of the size of the OE vocabulary we must bear several considerations in mind. (1) The total vocabulary of NE, as recorded, with some approach to completeness, in the largest of the most recent dictionaries, is, as compared with other languages both ancient and modern, uniquely, prodigiously, and indeed absurdly huge: the average Englishman today probably uses, ordinarily, no more words than the average Frenchman or German, but he quite certainly uses a smaller fraction of the total recorded and recognized vocabulary of his language. Accordingly, when we say that the OE vocabulary was small, we mean small relatively to that of NE – not nearly so small relatively to that of most other modern languages. (2) The OE vocabulary is certainly very incompletely recorded: extant OE documents are comparatively few and short, and limited in range of subject matter and genre, and lack, more or less by chance, instances of thousands of words that must have actually (even though perhaps only rarely) been used.[1] (3) The OE vocabulary of *c.* A.D. 1050 was much larger, more various, more precise, more subtle, and more easily expansible than that of about two hundred years earlier.

Let us consider the reasons for this last fact. There are just three ways of increasing the vocabulary of any language: (1) Forming absolutely new words arbitrarily (a method certainly not used, at least in historical times, on any important scale, but properly and even necessarily mentioned here for logical reasons); (2) assembling old words or other significant elements (e.g., *un-*, *-ly*) in new combinations – i.e., making new compound words; (3) borrowing words from other languages. NE uses chiefly method 3. It also uses method 2; but in practice far more new compounds in NE are made up of borrowed words

---

[1] The same is true, for that matter, of NE and of almost any language in any period. And the fragmentary and accidental way in which the OE vocabulary is recorded is additionally indicated by the hundreds of OE words that are found only once in surviving documents, though all of them must once have been in common or fairly common use.

and other elements (chiefly Latin and Greek) than of native
ones.[1] OE, also, had many loan-words – a handful from Celtic,
and a very large number – several hundreds – from Latin (many
of which had been earlier borrowed by Latin from Greek, and,
a few of them, from other languages). But (1) the hundreds of
Latin words in OE seem very few compared with the tens of
thousands in NE; (2) OE usually borrowed whole and individual
Latin words – it did not, i.e., as NE commonly does, very often
borrow formative elements (prefixes, suffixes, 'roots') and with
them construct, as NE commonly does, English compounds made
up of Latin elements but undreamt of by the Romans, nor did it,
as a rule, very freely compound Latin elements with native ones
– as, again, NE commonly does; and (3) the number of Latin
words 'naturalized' in English by *c.* A.D. 1050 was very much
larger than the number naturalized three hundred years earlier.

The fact that we must realize is that OE, though (especially
as compared with NE) a fairly distinct and single entity in
inflexion, idiom, spelling, pronunciation, and even syntax, is
far from being so clearly so in vocabulary. Extant records of
OE extend from a little before 700 to a little after 1100; and the
range and subtlety of ideas demanding and receiving expression
in the English language (though by no means *by the English
people*) at the end of that period were very much greater than
at the beginning of it. They were greater, however, not so
much because England was considerably more civilized by *c.* 1100
than it had been some four hundred years earlier (though it
certainly was, as a whole), as because it had been much *less*
civilized at about the middle of that period. In the seventh and
eighth centuries, English literary culture – or rather the literary
culture of England – flowered in two quite different ways. Many
poems were composed in English, and still more were first
written down (and some have survived), on subjects drawn
partly from ancient Germanic heroic legend and partly from
the Christian mythos; but the really active and advanced literary
culture of England in those centuries – at least as far as it has
survived – was, as it was throughout Europe, in the form of
learned Latin prose, in which, indeed, Englishmen excelled. Later,

---

[1] NE may almost be said to have borrowed, at least potentially, the whole
Latin vocabulary, and a large part of the Greek.

especially in the ninth century, the Scandinavians raided and to a considerable extent settled in England for the most part north and east of a line approximately from London to Liverpool, with the result that the Latin – and very secondarily the English – literary culture of England was wiped out north and east of that line, and, largely, south and west of it also. It was not till the time of Alfred, who came to the throne of Wessex *c.* 870 at the age of about twenty and died *c.* 900, that literary culture was revived in England, after a long period of darkness. Alfred himself tells us (in the preface to his – or his courtiers' – translation of St Gregory's *Cura Pastoralis*) that he ruled over a country to which, in times past, Continental Europeans had resorted (as indeed they had done a hundred years before) for Latin learning, but where now there were very few even of the clergy who could understand their daily Office in Latin. But, he continues, many can still read English[1] and many more can be easily taught to do so, and he has therefore resolved to translate or have his servants translate as many important Latin works into English as possible, in order that Christian learning may not utterly vanish from England.

Alfred largely carried out his plan, and the result was that, in the tenth and eleventh centuries, the practice of dealing *in vernacular prose* with sometimes quite abstruse subjects, and of accordingly moulding the vernacular to deal with them, was established in England to a degree beyond that yet realized in any other western European country: English was the first of all western European vernaculars, whether Germanic or Romance, to develop a polished literary prose. In order to acquire that distinction, it had to become refined and enriched; and the extent to which it became both is evident in the homilies and other works of Ælfric and Wulfstan, both ecclesiastics who died *c.* 1020, some 120 years after Alfred and some forty before the Norman Conquest. In their works, especially Ælfric's, the English language was filed and polished into what it had not been in the eighth century – a language that could do almost

---

[1] I.e., they knew their alphabet, and they knew their (spoken vernacular) language; and since spelling was practically phonetic, they were therefore able automatically to read and even write their language well enough for most practical purposes.

anything that Latin could do. This transformation showed itself chiefly in two ways: in a much more elaborate and flexible syntax (on the model of Latin) and in a much larger and more precise vocabulary. The increase in the vocabulary was brought about partly by borrowing a considerable number of Latin words, but only to something like the extent to which modern German has done so, and to nothing like the extent of NE or even ME. Instead, LOE increased its vocabulary chiefly as modern German has mainly done, viz., by making new compounds from elements of the native vocabulary. Compounds, to be sure, were nothing new in English: the poems of the eighth century are full of them. But the eighth-century poetic compounds tend to be mainly mere juxtaposition of two concrete nouns, whereas the typical compounds of the prose of the tenth and eleventh are rather verbs and abstract nouns formed by the various and ingenious use of adverbial prefixes, on the model of Latin – on that model, characteristically, to the extent of literally translating each successive element of a Latin compound into the corresponding English element.

The result was that OE of *c.* 1050 was a very different thing from that of about three hundred years before, though fundamentally it remained the same language (much more so than the language of a philosophical essay by Lord Russell, e.g., can be said to be in the same language as a seventeenth-century version of a popular ballad). And the paradoxical fact is that if Latin culture had not been for decades almost wiped out in England, and in England almost alone, English prose would almost certainly not have become a polished literary instrument long before every other western European vernacular, as it did – for Latin would have sufficed for Englishmen as it largely did for the nations of the Continent.

Chapter VIII

OLD ENGLISH DIALECTS

★

WE HAVE so far spoken of OE as if, however much it differed from time to time, it had always been, at any given time, uniform from place to place. That is not true: OE had its local dialects, as every language has. Disregarding minor differences, and minor dialects that must have existed but that we know little of, we may count four OE dialects: Kentish, West Saxon, Mercian, and Northumbrian. Kentish was spoken chiefly in what are now Kent and Surrey, and in the Isle of Wight, and was the language of the Jutes; West Saxon, in most of the rest of England south of the Thames and Bristol Channel;[1] Mercian,[2] the language of the southern Angles, from the Thames north to the Humber; and Northumbrian, the language of the northern Angles, from the Humber northward as far across the Scottish border as English was spoken. The dialects were pretty certainly already somewhat differentiated at the time of the Anglo-Saxon invasions. It is sometimes convenient to lump Mercian and Northumbrian together as 'Anglian', and, somewhat less often, to group them with Kentish as 'non-West Saxon'. Similarly, West Saxon and Kentish are sometimes conveniently spoken of together as Southern.

We know a good deal about the sounds and inflexions of all four dialects, but only of West Saxon have we many extensive continuous texts. The reason for this fact is as follows.

---

[1] Except in Cornwall, where a Celtic language continued to prevail for some centuries after the Anglo-Saxon conquest. It is interesting in this connexion to note that in the OE period Cornwall was often called West Wales, Wales proper being 'North Wales'. 'Wales' means 'the country of the Welsh', i.e., 'of the (especially Celtic) foreigners'; and 'Cornwall' means 'the Wales of the Cornovii' (a Celtic tribe living there).

[2] *Mercia* seems to have meant 'the marches', i.e., the frontier or border country, presumably so named from a Kentish or West Saxon point of view – a fact reflecting the earlier conquest, from the native Celts, of the south than of the midlands.

In the eighth century, the centre of English culture was in Northumbria;[1] but, as we have seen, Northumbrian culture was largely wiped out in the early part of the ninth century, and, at the end of that century, Wessex, with its capital at Winchester, and under the leadership of King Alfred, became the cultural centre. This shift had two effects: (1) A good deal of English literature produced in Northumbria and Mercia has been preserved only as 'translated' into West Saxon (though some recent scholars think that some literature that has been commonly supposed to have undergone that process was, rather, composed in a sort of compromise dialect); and (2) the West Saxon dialect became so firmly established as the normal language of English literature at the end of the ninth century that it retained that position in the tenth and eleventh and early twelfth, even after the political centre had travelled from Winchester to London and Westminster. Consequently, almost all extant OE literature (at least 'literary literature') is in West Saxon, and we must depend for our knowledge of non-West Saxon dialects of OE chiefly on what we can glean (1) from glosses[2] and charters, (2) from more or less accidental vestiges of the non-West Saxon dialects – imperfect translations, so to speak – in West Saxon transcriptions of non-West Saxon documents, (3) from the evidence of ME and NE dialects, and (4) from similar evidence in the forms of proper names of every period, especially place names.[3]

Probably the readiest way of appreciating the principal

[1] This may seem somewhat surprising considering that St Augustine arrived from Rome in Kent with his celebrated troop of missionaries in 597, and that his successors established less than seventy years later the Roman and Cantuarian hegemony as against the northern churches, which were partly indigenous British, partly founded by Irish and Scottish missionaries. The fact remains that till at least the early part of the ninth century the 'centre of English culture', at any rate in the sense 'centre of English-speaking and -writing culture', was in the north.

[2] Glosses, in the present connexion, are English equivalents of Latin words written between the lines of a Latin text – a 'pony' or 'trot', in effect.

[3] An illustration of both these latter kinds of evidence together may be found by investigating the NE words *weald* and *wold*, both meaning 'forest'. The prehistoric OE must have been **wald* [wɑld], and later (when most OE *a*'s ([ɑ]'s) had become *æ*'s ([æ]'s), **wæld* [wæld]. The vowel [ɑ]

differences between OE dialects is to look at two versions of
the opening lines of one of the few continuous literary OE texts
that have survived in two more or less pure dialectal forms,
viz., the celebrated 'Hymn of Cædmon' (the only poem of his
that is more or less certainly preserved), found in several mss
of Bede's *Ecclesiastical History of the English Nation* (both of
the original Latin and of the West Saxon translation of about
a hundred and fifty years later). On the left is a Northumbrian
text (the dialect of Cædmon and Bede), and on the right a West
Saxon. (Macrons are omitted.)

Nu *scy*lum hergan *hef*aenricaes uard	Nu *scu*lon herigean *heo*fonrices weard
metudaes *maecti* end his modgidanc	meotodes *meahte* & his modgepanc
uerc uuldor*f*adur *sue* he uundra gihuaes	*weorc* wuldor*fæ*der *swa* he wundra gehwæs
ec*i* dryctin or *asteli*dae.	ec*e* drihten or *onsteal*de.

is a back one, and [æ] front; and in West Saxon and Kentish the following
[1] was, clearly, a back consonant (or rather an 'inverted' one – one
produced by turning the tip of the tongue backward and upward).
As we have seen, in such a conjuncture one sound tends to modify the
other, and, in this case, the back [1] tended to generate a new back
vowel (a 'glide') between itself and the preceding front [æ]. The result
was something like [æə], which was conventionally spelt *ea* in West
Saxon, whence West Saxon *weald* [wæəld]. Later, in LOE or EME, two
things happened to this diphthong: (1) it became a monophthong, and
was sooner or later raised to [ɛ]; and (2) it lengthened, as short vowels
generally did before [ld] (and certain other sequences), to [ɛ:]. Finally,
ME [ɛ:] became ENE [e] and then LNE (Late Modern English) [i], and
thus we have the *Weald* [wild] of Kent, Surrey, and Sussex. (It is true
that this form was, apparently, in a sense revived by the sixteenth-century
antiquarian William Lambarde, but it still illustrates the regular development.) In Mercian, on the other hand, the [1] was apparently not a
particularly back or inverted sound, and hence produced no such diphthong;
and further, [æ] in Mercian tended to revert to [ɑ], whence Mercian
[wɑld]. But in Mercian, as well as in West Saxon and Kentish, most short
vowels, including [ɑ], lengthened before [ld], and [wɑld] thus became
[wɑ:ld] in LOE or EME. In later ME, except in the far north, [ɑ:] was
'backed', raised, and rounded to [ɔ], which subsequently became, in NE,
[o]; and thus we have the Chesney *Wold* of *Bleak House*.

The differences in spelling give an exaggerated impression of the differences in pronunciation, which were probably non-existent or negligible except in the italicized syllables, and which even in these would not have prevented mutual understanding.

This is probably the most appropriate place at which to say something more of this famous poem (the whole, incidentally, is only nine lines long), and of its alleged author. All we know of Cædmon is what Bede tells us in his *Ecclesiastical History*, book 4, chapter 22. According to Bede, Cædmon, an illiterate cowherd at Whitby Abbey in Yorkshire, in the days of the Abbess St Hild or Hilda (614–680), was commanded by a man in a dream to do what he had never done before – sing a song (i.e., compose impromptu, and recite, a poem), the subject to be the creation of the world. 'And straightway', says Bede, 'he began to recite in praise of God the Establisher verses that he had never heard, and of which this is the sense: "Now should we praise" ' – remember that this is all, including the poem, translated from Bede's Latin prose, not from Cædmon's (?) verse as given above – ' "the author of the heavenly kingdom, the power of the creator and his wisdom, the deeds of the father of glory. How he, as he is the everlasting God, stands forth as the author of all wonders. . . ." This,' Bede resumes, 'is the sense but not the actual arrangement of the words . . ., for poems, however well composed, cannot be translated literally from one language into another without impairing their beauty. . . .' Bede, it is clear from his original Latin text, did not himself (at least at first) reproduce Cædmon's original OE. But that original either was independently preserved – or, as is much less likely, was, so to speak, conjecturally restored – and was later inserted, in place of Bede's Latin prose paraphrase, in no fewer than seventeen extant mss of the *Ecclesiastical History*. Oddly enough, of these seventeen OE texts of the poem, all four in the original Northumbrian dialect are found in *Latin* mss (as are eight of those in West Saxon), the remaining five (also West Saxon) being in mss of the West Saxon translation of the *History*. The scribes or 'editors' of the mss (both Latin and English) containing the poem in English were logically obliged to omit or emend Bede's statement about the impossibility of satisfactory translations of poetry; they do so with varying degrees of completeness and neatness. The texts printed above represent (Northumbrian) ms KK. v. 16, Cambridge University Library, and (West Saxon) ms Tanner 10, Bodleian Library, and are taken from E. van K. Dobbie, *The Manuscripts of Cædmon's Hymn and Bede's Death Song*, N.Y., Columbia University Press, 1937, pp. 13 and 24. For more about Cædmon, or rather about his subsequent reputation, see the next chapter. Bede's Latin translation, incidentally, as retranslated here into NE, is not altogether exact; the OE may be more accurately rendered as 'Now we should praise the *guardian* of the heavenly kingdom, the power of the creator and his wisdom, the deeds of the father of glory. How he, the everlasting *Lord, established the beginning* of every wonder.'

Chapter IX

OLD ENGLISH LITERATURE

★

WHEN we first conceive such an entity as 'OE literature', our habits of thought and speech lead us almost inevitably to conceive it as having roughly the same relation to Anglo-Saxon culture and society as NE literature has to modern English culture and society – a relation with which we are fairly well acquainted. The brutal fact is that it has not the same relation. And the brutality of this fact is aggravated by further facts: (1) The OE literature that is extant is a very small part of the English literature produced in Anglo-Saxon times. (2) Much of that literature, especially of the poetry, that has been preserved, has been preserved in single mss, whose survival is almost purely a matter of chance. (3) Almost none of these single mss is either the author's autograph or an immediate copy of it; i.e., far more OE literature was produced (and copied and recopied) than has come down to us, and we have no assurance that what has come down to us is accurately and proportionately representative of the total amount produced or of its form and subject matter. (4) We have equally little assurance that what is preserved includes the best of what was produced. (5) We are used to thinking of literature as essentially someting *written*, as indeed the word *literature* properly implies; but there was certainly a great deal of OE 'literature' that was not written at all, but only composed 'in the head', and memorized and recited (first by the poet, later by professional *diseurs* – roughly speaking, minstrels), at first without so much as the conception of writing, though a small part eventually got written, and a small part of that small part has come down to us, as has a fair amount written more or less in imitation of it. (6) We are used to thinking of a people's literature as composed in their vernacular: English writers write English for other Englishmen to read; but much – one could almost say most – of what we may call the intellectually advanced and sophisticated literature produced by Englishmen, in England, for English readers, not only in the OE period but also in the ME, was in Latin (and, in the ME period, in French). (7) If we define 'literature' broadly enough, the potential and to a large extent the actual 'public' for English literature today embraces a very large fraction of the population: i.e., most English-speaking people can and on occasion do read English, and the enormous size, both relative and absolute, of the whole potential reading public profoundly affects the substance and the form of NE 'literature' in the broad sense of that term. But in the OE period (and in the ME), none of these things, certainly, were true. (8) People today have much to read: printing and its sequels have made books cheap and hence plentiful, and have done so for so long that we can hardly help overlooking the facts that, until comparatively recent times, (a) few Englishmen could read, (b) far fewer of them *did* read, and (c) even *they* had less to read, at least in English – which was all that most of them *could* read. 'Literacy' in the middle ages, both early and late, usually meant the ability to read (and often to write) Latin, not the mere understanding of the alphabet. (9) In NE, prose vastly exceeds verse in bulk, even in what can be called literature in the narrow sense, i.e., *belles lettres;* in OE, this was not true, or at least is not true of the surviving OE literature that is now most highly esteemed. (10) In the NE of at any rate the last couple of centuries, within the range of what we might call ' "more or less" *belles lettres*', the unquestionably and increasingly dominant form is the novel, or at least prose fiction; in OE, this was certainly far from true, though perhaps not to the extent suggested by the fact that exactly one independent and important piece of OE prose fiction (and that was a translation) survives today, viz., a version of the post-classical Greek story of Apollonius of Tyre – another version of which supplied much later the plot of Shakespeare's (?) *Pericles*. I.e., so far as we can judge from extant OE writings and from a general impression of life in the OE period – or almost any age before the last century or two – popular entertainment was not an important object of most writers or of most copyists of mss, whereas it certainly *is* the *most* important object of most creators and disseminators of modern printed books. (11) The range of subject matter of NE literature is very great, even in the narrow sense of 'literature'.

Surviving OE literature, on the other hand, especially poetry, is mainly restricted to subjects martial and heroic (and sometimes prehistoric and legendary) and (more especially in the later period) religious and ecclesiastical. (12) We are today used to thinking of 'English literature' as a continuous development: the literature of the twentieth century obviously grows out of that of the nineteenth, that of the nineteenth out of that of the eighteenth, and so on back. But OE literature had comparatively little effect on ME, and still less on NE: in all but one or two ways, the intellectual history of English-*speaking* culture – i.e., English cultural activity as recorded in vernacular documents – is pretty sharply broken off at the Norman Conquest.

In the light of all this, we may understand that, when we speak of 'OE literature', we are necessarily speaking of a concept different from 'NE literature' in almost every possible way. All we can do, in such a situation, is to observe the range and emphases of such OE literature as happens to remain, and learn such lessons from the facts as we can, without fancying that we can legitimately suppose the proportion 'OE literature : OE life :: NE literature : NE life'.

And this book, it happens, is not the place for anything like a really informative and illuminating descriptive and critical survey of surviving OE literature. The series of which this book is a part is called *The Language Library*, not 'the history of English literature', and the scale on which the book is designed will not permit a penetrating excursion into English literary history, the proper subject of other books, of which several deal with it admirably (see the reading list). Still, we may profitably spend a few pages here in a very brief summary.

Of OE verse, we have about 30,000 lines, from many poets of some three centuries – hardly as much as we have from Chaucer alone in the fourteenth century. Practically all this verse is in the ancient Germanic alliterative form. What is 'the ancient Germanic alliterative form'?

To answer this question we must consider the several forms in which what we can agree to call verse is composed. We may first leave out of consideration here the kind of 'verse' exemplified by most ancient Hebrew poetry (e.g., the Psalms in the original language), where the balance or alternation that perhaps essentially distinguishes verse from prose is mainly rhetorical: consists, i.e., mainly in a balance of ideas and to some extent constructions rather than of words. Secondly, we may put out of account the 'free verse' of our own time, which, at best, is verse only in a very subtle way, and, at worst, in no discernible way at all.

This leaves us, practically speaking, with verse definable as words (making, or presumably intended to make, sense) arranged according to some fairly definite rhythmical pattern recurring in what are in some way recognized as units, commonly called 'lines'. The rhythmical pattern may be determined in four ways: (1) By the distribution of literally long and short syllables, i.e., quantitative verse; (2) by the mere number of syllables in a line; (3) by a combination of number of syllables with number and distribution of stressed (i.e., practically, 'loud') and (relatively) unstressed syllables; (4) by number and distribution of stressed syllables, with hardly any regard to the number of syllables generally. Classical Greek and Latin verse exemplify no. 1; typical verse in most of the Romance languages exemplifies sometimes no. 2, sometimes a moderate degree of no. 3; typical NE verse exemplifies an advanced degree of no. 3 – often so advanced as to approach no. 4; OE verse exemplifies no. 4 in its full degree.

Besides number, and relative length or loudness, of syllables, European verse often, as of course we all know, uses rhyme, i.e., identical sounds at the ends of lines, but ancient Germanic (including OE) verse used instead what may be called 'initial rhyme' (as distinguished from rhyme in the familiar sense, or 'end rhyme'), but is more often called alliteration, which means simply that metrically prominent or governing syllables, or most of them, begin with the same or similar sounds. We are all familiar with alliteration as an occasional effective literary device in modern literature and sometimes as an accidental blemish or deliberate joke – 'Around the rough and rugged rocks the ragged rascal ran' – but we do not commonly use it as a structural principle of verse. Ancient Germanic (including OE) verse did.

The fundamental unit of OE verse is a line containing four

strongly stressed[1] syllables, two in each half of the line. The number of unstressed syllables in each half-line may vary from two (or, in very special circumstances, one) up to a theoretically almost unlimited number, though in practice the limit in normal lines is about eight, and the average about four. The whole line is bound together by the use of the same sound, or approximately or originally the same sound, at the beginning of at least one syllable in each half-line – usually the first in each half, but often also the second in the first half. I.e., if we call a stressed and alliterated syllable 'a', and a stressed but not alliterated one 'x', the commonest patterns are 'a x a x' and 'a a a x', though there are others.

We cannot go into further detail here about the ins and outs of OE alliterative verse, but let us look at an example, the most famous lines in surviving OE poetry – the opening sentence of the longest and best known and greatest extant OE poem, *Beowulf*. Each line is presented in three forms: (1) The OE text, with the metrically stressed syllables italicized; (2) a phonetic transcription representing as nearly as possible the theoretical pronunciation of early tenth-century West Saxon; (3) a NE translation as literal as is practical.

Hwæt, wē *Gār-De*na in *gēarda*gum,

   [hwæt we ˈgɑːrˈdɛnɑ ɪn ˈjæːrˈdɑɣʊm]

   Lo, we, of the Spear-Danes in yore-days,

*þēodcyn*inga *þrym* gefrūnon,

   [ˈθeədˈkynɪŋgɑ ˈθrym jɛˈfrunɒn]

   of the(ir) folk-kings, the fame have heard,

hū ðā *æþeling*as *el*len *freme*don.

   [hu θɑː ˈæðɛˈlɪŋgɑs ˈɛllɛn ˈfrɛmɛdɒn]

   how the nobly-descended (ones) deeds-of-valour wrought.

---

[1] The pre-eminence of stress (i.e., loudness) over quantity (i.e., literal duration of syllables) and also over pitch (i.e., literal musical 'highness' or 'lowness'), as a means of giving certain syllables prominence over others, is one of the notable marks of Germanic as against primitive IE, and to a large extent also as against most of the other branches of the IE stock, and probably accounts in part for several of the peculiarities of the Germanic languages. But why the Germanic languages should have developed this fondness for stress in the first place is not known, though there are one or two interesting theories.

Beowulf by itself constitutes more than a tenth part of all the OE verse that survives, and it has come down to us in just one ms. This latter fact is true of all but a few OE poems, the great majority of which, furthermore, are found in one or another of four codices,[1] all preserved by happy accident, and worthy of being named, as the most precious and venerable relics of our earliest literature: (1) The ms containing *Beowulf* and one other (fragmentary) poem, *Judith* – ms Cotton Vitellius A. xv.[2] (2) The 'Exeter Book', so called from having been, apparently since 1072, in the library of Exeter Cathedral, to which it was almost certainly presented by Bishop Leofric, who died in that year. (3) The 'Vercelli Book', so called from its presence in the library of the Cathedral of Vercelli, some forty miles west of Milan. How or when it made its astounding journey to that place has been the subject of much conjecture, some of it wild, but not wilder than the indisputable fact of its presence there for an undetermined number of centuries. (4) The 'Junius ms' (now in full 'Bodleian ms Junius XI', at Oxford), so named from

[1] Codices (singular, codex) are books of the modern shape as distinguished from scrolls.

[2] This designation indicates that this ms, like so many other very notable ones, many of them OE, forms part of the collection of the antiquarian Sir Robert Bruce Cotton (1571–1631). The Cottonian collection was presented to the nation by Cotton's grandson in 1700, suffered grievously in 1731 from a fire at Ashburnham House, where it was then kept, and was removed in 1753 to the British Museum, where it still is. Sir Robert arranged his collection in a number of bookcases of which twelve were surmounted each by the bust of a Roman emperor, and designated the several shelves of each case by letters of the alphabet and each codex by a number, and these designations have been kept ever since. 'Ms Cotton Vitellius A. xv' therefore means 'the fifteenth volume on the top shelf of the case surmounted by a bust of the Emperor Vitellius'. If Sir Robert had not been the zealous collector that he was, our knowledge of OE literature would probably be even more – very much more – fragmentary than it is; few of his contemporaries united the interest, the knowledge, the opportunities, and the resources requisite to making and preserving intact such a collection as he made. The only regrettable fact about his career is that he was not born a hundred years sooner: the remains of Early English literature would be incalculably richer if he had been.

having been acquired in the middle of the seventeenth century
by the remarkable Franciscus (or Franz) Junius, or François du
Jon *le jeune* (1589–1677), French by ancestry, German by birth,
Dutch by education, and English by long residence (1621–1651
and 1675–1677): one of the greatest early students (though
there were some a hundred years earlier) of Early English and
the early Germanic dialects generally.

Junius not only owned the ms: he read it, studied it, and in
1654 became the first publisher of the four poems in it, now
known as *Genesis, Exodus, Daniel,* and *Christ and Satan,* all on
the biblical or quasi-biblical themes suggested by the titles, and
all of them, except the last, mainly paraphrases, in one degree
or another, of parts of the biblical books of the same names.
They were supposed – and represented – by Junius to be the
works of the eighteenth-century poet Cædmon (on the basis of
Bede's description of Cædmon's poems), but the present state
of opinion regarding that attribution is shown by the general
practice of referring to the first three as at most 'Cædmonian'.

The last of the four poems, *Christ and Satan,* stands apart
from the rest in being, in the words of a recent editor, 'more in
the manner of Cynewulfian than in that of Cædmonian verse'.[1]
This quotation naturally leads to some mention of Cynewulf,
the only OE poet of whose works we certainly possess more than
a single one and, except for Cædmon, the only certainly very
productive one whose name we know. Further, we know that
name only because Cynewulf, alone among surviving OE poets,
took the pains, as we have seen earlier, to 'sign' four poems by
inserting the runic letters of his name inextricably into the text.[2]
But his name is almost everything we do know about him: we

---

[1] G. P. Krapp, ed., *The Junius Manuscript,* N.Y., Columbia University
Press, 1931, p. xxxv.

[2] This means of insuring the accreditation of a work to an author may
seem to us oddly laborious and tortuous and mannered and quaint and even
perverse, but Cynewulf knew what he was about. Under the conditions of
book production and preservation before printing, it was hardly safe for
an author to rest the perpetuation of his fame on a title page at the beginning of his autograph or on an *explicit* or the like at the end: scribes were
too prone to regard the author's name as unimportant, and first and last
leaves were too likely to become detached from the codex.

cannot even say with certainty in what century he lived (except that it was the eighth or ninth) or in what part of England (except that it was pretty certainly not the south). The four signed poems (he may also be the author of other extant ones, unsigned) are commonly called *The Ascension of Christ*, *Juliana* (a saint's life) – both in the Exeter Book – *The Fates of the Apostles*, and *Elene* (the tale of the Invention of the Cross) – both in the Vercelli.

Most surviving OE poems are, like the Cædmonian and Cynewulf's, religious in one way or another, though there are some that are rather merely moral and some elegiac, and also a number of odds and ends of various less important kinds. The one other really important (but much smaller) class is the martial and heroic, of which *Beowulf* is much the longest and most noteworthy. *Beowulf* itself, and a few others, draw their material largely from the great stock of pre-Christian common Germanic legend, and thus represent earlier material, though they were by no means all of them necessarily composed in their present form at an earlier date, than the religious poems glanced at above; and a martial poem or two, imitating the style and to some extent the atmosphere of *Beowulf*, etc., but dealing with contemporary events, were composed in the tenth and eleventh centuries. The preservation of any such pre-Christian, not to say un-Christian, material as is found in *Beowulf*, in a self-consciously Christian age by self-consciously Christian scribes, is remarkable; but far more must have been allowed to perish than has been preserved, and even *Beowulf* exhibits, in its present form, a decidedly Christian colouring, to which indeed it may owe its preservation.[1]

As for OE prose, most of it is later than most of the verse, as in most national literatures.[2] The two great names in OE prose

[1] It is not meant to imply here that the existing poem called *Beowulf* was in the main composed by a pre-Christian pagan and then recast and interpolated by a Christian successor, but only that most of the raw material is pre-Christian and pagan, and some of the rest of it at least not peculiarly Christian.

[2] The most important reason for this general fact is that, in a preliterate age, when 'literature' is necessarily oral, memorized, and recited, verse, as being easier to memorize, is naturally the dominant form. We must also remember the magical and incantatory impression that verse is likely to make on the unsophisticated mind; cf. nursery rhymes.

are King Alfred and the Abbot Ælfric, both of whom we have had occasion to mention before. It will probably remain forever quite uncertain how many of the English translations from Latin attributed to Alfred are actually his work: some of them were certainly, and most of them probably, 'his' only in the sense of having been commissioned, promoted, and perhaps to some extent overseen by him. An occasional original passage inserted here and there in some of these translations is, however, probably really his, notably the preface to the translation of St Gregory's *Cura Pastoralis*, already quoted. Besides this work, the 'Alfredian' translations include some of Gregory's *Homilies*, Orosius's *Universal History*, Boethius's *Consolation of Philosophy*, and Bede's *Ecclesiastical History of the English Nation*. As for original composition in OE prose, King Alfred was probably also the instigator of the *Anglo-Saxon Chronicles* (a better name than the usual 'Anglo-Saxon Chronicle', since all the extant texts differ in many places despite their large amount of common material).

From Ælfric we have, besides many saints' lives and other homilies and a number of miscellaneous works, a translation (his in part only) of the Heptateuch and a treatise on the Bible, and there is also an anonymous translation of the Gospels (from which we have seen a passage some chapters earlier). From Ælfric's colleague Wulfstan we have four sermons; from many anonymous writers, considerable numbers of homilies and saints' lives, and odds and ends of several kinds, including even some scientific writing. The solitary relic of OE prose fiction that is both fairly long and evidently written for sheer entertainment, without ulterior didactic intent, *Apollonius of Tyre*, has already been mentioned.

These few paragraphs, it should be repeated, do not pretend to be anything like an adequate survey of extant OE literature; their object has been only to give some very general idea of its range and quantity. It will be well, however, not to leave the subject without mentioning two important facts about the style of much OE prose, both of them serviceable in keeping us from supposing that that prose was characteristically naïve and crude. These are (1) that in a good deal of it – particularly in Ælfric's homilies – the style closely approaches the rhythmic and alliterative patterns and the extensive use of ornamental synonyms and epithets of OE verse; and (2) that in much of it – again, especially in Ælfric – the figures and patterns of post-classical Latin rhetoric are extensively imitated. We have here an interesting conjunction of the most admired and most obviously appropriate and available foreign models with almost the only native ones having any ancient prestige.

Chapter X

'1066 AND ALL THAT'

★

THE NORMAN CONQUEST of England in the usual sense – military and political – was sudden and violent; but the Norman, or rather the French, conquest of England in the cultural sense was neither sudden and violent, nor so late in beginning, nor so accidental. French influence in this respect began in England some decades before 1066, and would certainly have continued and grown without any 'conquest' at all. Edward the Confessor, the last 'Anglo-Saxon' King of England (discounting two reigns occupying between them less than a year), was the son of an English father, indeed, but of a Norman mother, and, what is more important, was taken as a child to the Norman court, where he stayed for nearly thirty years, and where he acquired French ideas and tastes, the French language, and French friends, and his sister acquired a French husband, who became one of his royal brother-in-law's French friends to such good purpose that Edward supported him in a quarrel with English magnates. Another French friend was an ecclesiastic, Robert of Jumièges, whom Edward brought with him to England on his return there to mount the throne, and, as soon as possible, made Bishop of London (1044) and later Archbishop of Canterbury (1051). He also may have made, at about the latter date, some sort of (at least extralegal) bequest of the throne (he was childless) to his Norman first cousin, the bastard William (later 'the Conqueror'), as William asserted; the two cousins' relations, at any rate, were certainly close and friendly, and the English King belonged decidedly to the Francophile party in English politics. Even if the 'bequest' was never made, or if, having been made, it had never been enforced by William, French cultural influence had begun and would pretty certainly have continued and increased.

But it would hardly have come to exercise so profound an effect on the English language, which would almost certainly be today in most ways a very different thing from what it is if only Edward the Confessor had had a son, or even a daughter. The effect on the language was the indirect result of the rapid and almost complete Normanizing, or rather Gallicizing, of the ruling class. Within five years of the Battle of Hastings, William had, with grim and cynical despatch and thoroughness, dispossessed nearly all the important native landowners in favour of his Norman (and other French) accomplices. What was at least immediately more important in its bearing on the language and literature of England, he did the same thing in the Church (as, under mediaeval conditions, was a matter of course): ten years after the Conquest, of the fourteen episcopal sees then in existence (William founded three more during his reign), just three were still held by English bishops, and, by William's death in 1087, just one. Much the same thing happened with the great abbacies – more important in some ways, culturally speaking, than the bishoprics. In short, before the end of the eleventh century, the throne, the royal administration, education, almost all the agricultural land (and hence almost all the wealth and economic power), and all the great places in the Church and many of the small ones were possessed by men of French birth, French culture, and French language. French had become within three decades inevitably the daily language, both spoken and written, of nine out of every ten of the persons of weight and substance in England.

This is not to say that English ceased altogether to be written, and by men of some considerable culture and standing; to mention only one instance, the Anglo-Saxon Chronicle as kept at Peterborough Minster was continued until, or rather was resumed after an interval, as late as 1154, and in a form of English hardly more different from that of a hundred years before than it would have been, Conquest or no Conquest; and even *belles lettres*, even poetry, continued in a thin stream. But the stream was very thin indeed, at least to judge from extant documents, and not till *c.* 1300 or even later does it begin to become once more a prominent feature of the still discernible cultural landscape of England. Meanwhile, most books written in England (at least so far as they have been preserved) were in (Norman-)French or Latin, for the very good reason that those were the languages generally esteemed and ordinarily used by this or that section of the dominant and influential classes, who almost alone read or were even very commonly read to.

And yet, of course, English survived – survived as the only language of the great mass of the population of England and as, doubtless, the occasional spoken language of most of their betters, nor did it, as the colloquial (and virtually only) language of the populace at large, change a great deal more or faster, probably, than it would have, whether or not *literary* OE had remained dominant in *literature*, or whether or not French (and Latin) had succeeded it in that capacity. The impression that one gets of unexpectedly great changes between the English of *c.* 1000 and that of *c.* 1200 is largely owing to the fact that most surviving English documents of the later period use a language descended not from the literary OE of the earlier but from the colloquial – and more or less lower-class or at least familiar and domestic and everyday – which must even in the tenth and eleventh centuries have been more different from the contempo-rary sophisticated and literary than the language of a London bus-driver today is from that of a leading article in *The Times*.

This popular colloquial OE was certainly already exhibiting, well before the Conquest, a tendency not, indeed, operative equally always and everywhere, but still one very common in the development of most languages – the tendency first to con-found and then to slough off distinctions, especially in inflexional syllables, that have come for one reason or another to be or seem superfluous, and also gradually to alter pronunciation partly by slurring and partly by the operation of 'phonetic drift'. These tendencies were not limited, even before the Conquest, to the spoken language of the common people; they are evident in LOE literary documents. But until the Conquest, the existence and continued written use of a more or less standard literary English had the usual effect of moderating and retarding these chiefly popular colloquial tendencies towards change (though pretty certainly not to the extent suggested by the surviving literary documents, whose various and extensive vocabulary and elaborate and subtle syntax had never been shared by the people at large, and which continued to use inflexions and seemingly indicate a pronunciation that had certainly in large measure ceased to be so shared). With the sudden displacement of English as the normal upper-class and literary language, however, and its relegation, in the main, to lower-class and merely utilitarian purposes, the changes already under way were naturally accelerated, with the result that the typical English document of *c.* 1200 is startlingly more different from one of two centuries earlier than we should expect it to be.

Most literary EME, i.e., is based on popular colloquial LOE, not on literary, and it reflects a number of very important traits of that mode of speech. (1) Popular colloquial LOE had largely lost, if indeed it had ever made much use of, the power of free, flexible, and imaginative compounding of new words out of native elements; (2) it had lost, if it had ever had, large numbers of words whether simple or compound, many of which, at least, seem to have been, even in the days of their currency, only or at any rate mainly poetic or upper-class or learned; (3) it had simplified and regularized and vulgarized its inflexions and sounds; (4) it had complicated and multiplied its dialectal variations and divisions. The deficiencies of this language for literary and otherwise sophisticated purposes were made good, for the most part, not by reviving the shape and 'machinery' of literary OE, but by enriching and refining colloquial EME through loans from and imitations of French and Latin. This was almost inevitable because most EME writers were accustomed to writing, and often speaking and even thinking in, French or Latin rather than English, particularly in connexion with all but the most ordinary affairs of daily life. Thus, (1) compounds once more became common, but they are now made up mainly and often wholly of French and Latin elements or are, even oftener, borrowed from those languages ready-made; (2) great numbers of simple (i.e., uncompounded) French and Latin words are borrowed; (3) the simplification of inflexion is kept from reducing intelligibility by the use of a comparatively rigid word order; (4) the subtlety and exactness with which distinctions in tenses of verbs may be expressed are greatly enhanced over anything that either colloquial or literary OE had to offer, and enhanced by the imitation of Latin models; (5) the long-accumulating changes in pronunciation are now so to speak officially recognized and revealed by adapting to the representation of the sounds of English words the conventions of contemporary French spelling – a spelling which, once we understand it, is much more effectually phonetic (for ME) than LOE spelling had come to be.

Between ME and NE there has been no breach of continuity comparable to that between OE and ME (for the good reason that never since EME has English undergone any such literary submergence as it did between LOE and EME), particularly in spelling and in the general appearance of the written language; on the other hand, just because that is so – just because ME looks so much more like NE than OE does – we are likely to be misled in two ways: (1) we are likely not to realize that, though ME looks more like NE than it does like OE, it sounded fundamentally more like OE than it does like NE;[1] and (2) we are likely not to realize that many words still current in NE were used in very different senses in ME. It is easier for us, in short, to misunderstand ME than OE (when we understand or think we understand the latter at all), just because we don't expect it to be so: e.g., when Chaucer says of the Knight in the General Prologue to the *Canterbury Tales* that 'he loved *chivalrye,/ Trouthe* and honour, *fredom* and *curteisie*'; that he was 'ful *worthy* in his lordes werre'; that '*therto* had he *riden,* no man ferre'; that he had often been the guest of honour at knightly banquets in East Prussia 'aboven alle *nacions*'; that 'he hadde a soverayn *prys*'; and that he had never in his life said any '*vilenye*' to anyone – not one of the italicized words means quite what it means today.[2] And these words, like any passage in Chaucer or ME generally, are deceptive to the NE reader in another way, viz., that they were certainly pronounced much less nearly as they are today than the not very great differences in spelling suggest.

At this point we find ourselves in something of a dilemma. It is not easy to consider the leading differences in sounds, inflexions, and spelling between OE and ME generally without some preliminary notion of ME dialects, and it is not easy to

---

[1] An excellent example is afforded by OE *scrūd*, ME *shroud*, and NE *shroud*. The OE and ME are spelt differently but had the same sound, [ʃruːd]; the NE, though spelt exactly like the ME, is pronounced [ʃraud].

[2] Unconnected with this fact, but still decidedly proper matter for remark here, is the fact, characteristic of at least LME, that, of these ten words, no fewer than half are French loan-words.

consider ME dialects without some preliminary notion of the leading differences between OE and ME generally. But we must make a choice; and on the whole, illogical as it may seem and unsatisfactory as it in some ways certainly is, the first-mentioned order – general changes before dialects – is the more practical. But in order to make it as practical as possible, we must in some sort compromise by taking a particular ME dialect at a particular period as our standard of comparison with OE (which itself, after all, was not, as we have seen, a uniform entity either geographically or chronologically, though it can in practice be treated as much more nearly so than ME by taking West Saxon of the tenth century – essentially the language of the great majority of surviving OE documents – as the standard). For a number of reasons, our 'standard' ME for the immediate purposes will be what is called the South-east Midland dialect (henceforth SEM) of the late fourteenth century – i.e., virtually the language of Chaucer. There is, to be sure, one way in which this is most inconvenient, viz., that the ME of Chaucer is not the direct descendant of the OE of (at least the present text of) *Beowulf* or King Alfred or Ælfric, so that a good deal about Chaucer's ME cannot be explained by reference to their OE. This, however, is the fault of history. We have already seen that the first efflorescence of English literature was in the Northumbrian dialect, but that, again for historical reasons, most extant OE documents are in West Saxon (and often the West Saxon of a century or two or three later than the composition of the works), so that we are practically obliged to base most of our ideas about the OE of all times and regions on the OE of Wessex in the tenth century. The centre of vernacular culture shifted, i.e., in the ninth century from the northern to the south-central part of England. In the same way, even before the Conquest, owing to the absorption of the Scandinavian invaders early in the eleventh century and to the consequently restored political unity of England, London and Westminster[1] could and did resume

---

[1] We may here well remind ourselves that St Edward, King and Confessor, acquired the saintly part of his title largely because he rebuilt Westminster Abbey – as a part of his rehabilitation of the City of Westminster as the chief seat of royal authority. The new building was completed barely in time to receive the Royal Saint's corpse.

their natural place as the centre of national life; and though, for so long as OE continued to be cultivated as a literary language – i.e., for nearly a century after the Conquest – the West Saxon dialect maintained its prestige as a quasi-national literary standard, it was inevitable that it should be displaced from that eminence by the dialect of London sooner or later. The Conquest probably hastened the displacement, but did not cause it: before Chaucer's death the London dialect (basically a variety of SEM) was already fast approaching the status of a national literary and official norm, a status which it has long since come to occupy fully and firmly.[1]

---

[1] On this point three observations should be made. (1) It is sometimes (less often now than formerly) said that the London dialect became the national standard because Chaucer used it; the fact is rather that Chaucer used it (a) because it was his native dialect, and (b) because it was already on its way to becoming the national standard – was already, in a very literal sense, 'the King's English', though doubtless Chaucer's unique prestige in the fifteenth century to some extent determined the vocabulary, idiom, and syntax of standard *literary* ENE. (2) London English of Chaucer's time has yielded (but see point 3 below) *standard literary* NE – i.e., its influence is paramount all over the English-speaking world in the vocabulary, idiom, and syntax of formal written English. In spoken English, on the other hand, and especially in 'familiar' and 'domestic' English, that influence is less powerful and sweeping. It is also less clearly perceptible, especially in everyday vocabulary and in pronunciation; to say that the London English of Chaucer's time is the source of standard NE is not to say that the London English of the twentieth century is the source, or even the model. (3) The London dialect of Chaucer's time is not in quite all respects (though it is in most) the direct ancestor of the London dialect of later centuries: in the course of the fifteenth and early sixteenth centuries, the dialect of London came to be a little less like that of Kent and a little more like that of most of Essex and Middlesex – came to be, i.e., more strictly SEM and less plainly SEM tinged with Kentish.

Chapter XI

HOW MIDDLE ENGLISH WAS SPELT
AND HOW IT SOUNDED

★

SEM ME of the late fourteenth century, like most ME, especially
LME, was spelt according to a system that owed little to OE and
almost everything to contemporary French. This is perfectly
natural considering how soon after the Conquest the intellectual
life of England was taken over by the French-speaking invaders,
and how almost completely and for how long a time it remained
in their hands. They knew little and cared less about traditional
English orthography, and applied to English, when they began
to write it, practically the entire orthography of their native
tongue. This French orthography differed from OE in two ways:
(1) it was less uniform – it used indifferently, i.e., more ways
of spelling this sound or that; and (2) it disguised the phonetic
identity, complete or nearly so, of many ME words with their
OE 'ancestors'. But let us see first precisely how the alphabet
is at least conventionally supposed to have been used, according
to this mainly French model, by Chaucer and his neighbours.

CONSONANTS

b, d, f, h, j, k, l, m, n, p, q, s (by itself), *t, v, w, x*, and *z* had
the values they usually have in NE. Note that ME adds to the
corresponding OE list *f, h, j*, and *v, f* having been in OE sometimes [f] but sometimes [v], *h* sometimes [h] but sometimes
[x], and *j* and *v* not having been distinguished from *i* and *u* in
either form or function.[1] ME also uses much more often than OE

---

[1] As a matter of fact, they were not commonly distinguished in form
even in ME, but a real difference (or rather multiplicity) in function had
come into being none the less: *i* sometimes means [dʒ] in ME, never in OE;
u sometimes means [v] in ME, seldom in OE (never in the 'classical' West
Saxon spelling of any but Latin words, especially proper names – e.g.,
'Dauides' in the OE version of *St Luke* ii in Chapter II, above).

the letters *k* (often for OE *c* even in the neighbourhood of back vowels), *q* (OE spelt [kw] *cw;* ME spells it *qu*), and *z.*

r, as in OE, was never 'silent' or 'dropped'.

c, by itself, had lost the value [tʃ] that it had come to have in OE in the neighbourhood of most front vowels, but it retained the value [k] in the neighbourhood of back ones, and acquired a new secondary value, [s], in the neighbourhood of front vowels – at first in French loan-words only, but later in some native ones. (E.g., OE *mȳs* ('mice') [my:s], EME (SEM) *mīs* or *mȳs* [mi:s], LME and ENE *mice* (but still [mi:s]), LNE still *mice,* but now [mais].) The sound [tʃ], represented by *c* in OE, occurred also in ME in both native and French words, but came to be represented by the French spelling *ch,* as it still usually is.

g must in ME, otherwise than in OE, be 'divided' into two forms, ʒ and *g* 'proper'. ʒ is called *ʒoʒ, yogh* [jox]. In form it is the OE (originally Irish) modification of Roman *G,* and it remained in ME use with both OE voiced fricative values, especially the front [j], the back voiced fricativ [ɣ] (which occurred rarely in ME) being at least as often spelt *gh* (as the voiceless correlative [x] was) in the French fashion. The name [jox] exemplifies both values. The form *g* is an importation from French, and, though originally the same as ʒ, is commonly used in ME as a distinct letter, with two values: (1) the voiced velar stop [g] in both native and French words, and (2) the post-alveolar affricate [dʒ], at first in French words but later also in native ones (where it was comparatively rare). This latter sound, when not initial, was often spelt *dg(e).* (It had been spelt *cg* in OE, as we have seen.)

gh. This is the usual ME way of indicating the velar fricative, both voiceless [x] – OE *h* (in certain positions) – and voiced [ɣ] – OE ʒ (i.e., *g*) (again, in certain positions); but [ɣ] was, as we have seen, rare in ME.

gn, kn, wr. In ME as in OE, both letters in these sequences were pronounced even when initial, as they have ceased to be in NE, though they are still written.

sh, ssh, sch, all French spellings, and sometimes *s, ss,* replaced the native *sc* in the value [ʃ], *sc* coming to indicate (again, in the French fashion) only [sk] in the neighbourhood of back vowels and [s] in that of front ones.

þ, ð. Of these two letters, the second disappeared almost entirely; the first continued to be used till the sixteenth century, and in a sort of distorted and limited way[1] even later (in handwriting if not in printing), but came more and more to be displaced by the digraph *th*.

w. As in NE, but see above under *kn*, and below under *wh* and also under *eu*.

wh is in ME as in NE the normal spelling of what OE spelt more sensibly *hw*. The native language of the Norman invaders of the eleventh century did not contain the sequence [hw], which, when they heard it in English, apparently seemed to them to be not so much [hw] as what might be called a voiceless [w]; and the spelling they contrived for this sound, *wh*, does not mean that they actually thought that [hw] was [wh], but was rather a way of saying 'this sound is an indefinably odd kind of *w*'.

y. As in NE, but see also under Vowels below.

VOWELS

Long

Long vowels in OE are sometimes distinguished in mss from short ones by acute accents (usually macrons in modern prints); in ME they practically never are, and in modern prints seldom. We may still usefully distinguish them, occasionally, on the basis of the etymology or subsequent pronunciation, and they are printed below with macrons, which should be understood, however, to be almost entirely modern and editorial.

[1] What is meant by this is that þ, in much of the handwriting of the fifteenth century, was formed very like *y*, so that early English printers, coming to England with type founded for printing French (which had no þ), very naturally used *y* for þ in printing English. The results of this practice are the frequent *ye* and *yt* (or better, *y^e* and *y^t*) for *the* and *that* in much handwriting even as late as the nineteenth century. This has led to such absurdities as pronouncing 'ye' in 'Ye Olde Coffee Shoppe' as [jiː] instead of as [ðiː] or [ðɪ], even when such phrases are printed (as they now usually are) rather than written by hand.

ā: [ɑ:]; e.g., *fāre*(*n*), 'to fare, to go', [ˈfɑ:rə(n)].[1]

ē. (1) [e]; e.g., *dēme*(*n*), 'to deem', [ˈdemə(n)]; (2) [ɛ:];
e.g., *lēde*(*n*), 'to lead', [ˈlɛ:də(n)]. (The sources of these two

[1] This is the conventional view, but the conventional view is probably
wrong, as we may see from the following facts. In very early NE all the
'long' vowels tended, for some mysterious reason, to rise by one step:
i.e., low vowels became mid, and mid vowels became high (or at least
higher mid), so that [ɔ] and [ɛ:] became respectively [o] and [e], and
the old [o] and [e] became [u] and [i]. This would by itself have resulted
in a falling together of the new and old [u]s and of the new and old [i]s,
but in point of fact the old [u] and [i], though they could not be raised
(being already as high as possible), did undergo a change, viz., diph-
thongization to (ultimately) [au] and [ai] respectively, thus leaving room,
so to speak, for the old [o] and [e] to replace them as [u] and [i]. But
among the OE long vowels, one and one only – *ā*[ɑ:] – seems, if we assume
that it was still [ɑ:] in SEM in Chaucer's time, as the conventional theory
does assume, to have moved two or even three steps, i.e., to have been
both fronted (to [a:] and then to [æ:]) and then raised (to [e]), while
all the other long vowels were moving only one step. This is inherently
unlikely: it is much more probable that ENE [e] (when spelt *ā* – e.g., in
name [nem]) derives immediately from LME [æ:] – by one step – rather
than from EME [ɑ:] – by two or even three steps at once; more probable,
i.e., that EME [ɑ:] had already been fronted to [æ:] in LME, or at least to
[a:], so that the resultant sound had only, or almost only, to be raised in
ENE to [e] – i.e., to take one step, along with all the other participants in
the 'great vowel shift', as this process is called, instead of two. This
fronting probably occurred very late, so that taking SEM *ā* as [ɑ:] up to,
say, *c*. 1300 or even a little later is probably right, but supposing that
Chaucer pronounced it as [ɑ:] rather than as [æ:] (or at least as [a:])
is probably wrong. Chaucer, i.e., probably said, in the first line of the
Canterbury Tales, something closer to [ˈæ:prɪl] ('Aprill') than to
[ˈɑ:prɪl], and, in the third, something closer to [ˈbæ:ðɪd] ('bathed')
than to [ˈbɑ:ðɪd]. And it should be added that the whole of the 'great
vowel shift' had probably entered its first stages during Chaucer's life-
time, so that, though the full modern system would certainly have sounded
to him so 'advanced' as to be always outlandish and sometimes unintelligible, the system presented above would, on the other hand, probably
have struck him as old-fashioned. But until further light is forthcoming, it
seems wise to stick fairly close to the conventional system. On all this,
as on everything below about Chaucer's pronunciation, see Helge
Kökeritz, *A Guide to Chaucer's Pronunciation*, Stockholm and New Haven
(Conn., U.S.A.), 1954.

values of ME *ē* are too various and complex to be discussed here.)
This second *ē* is often nowadays written *ę̄* by modern editors
and grammarians not using IPA symbols, and called 'open *ē*' in
distinction from the first sound, called 'close *ē*', for the good
reason that they actually differ in the width to which the mouth
is open – i.e., in height.

ī: [i]; e.g., *bīte(n)*, 'to bite', [ˈbitə(n)].

ō: (1) [o]; e.g., *bōte(n)*, 'to boot, to avail', [ˈbotə(n)]; (2)
[ɔ]; e.g., *ok*, 'oak', [ɔk]. In SEM of the late fourteenth century,
[ɔ] is usually derived from OE [ɑ:]; i.e., in this dialect and at
this time it was 'backed', raised, and rounded. In contemporary
northern ME, on the other hand, it remained [ɑ:]. This second
ō is often written *ǭ* and called 'open *ō*' as distinguished from the
first *ō*, called 'close *ō*', exactly as with the two values of *ē*.

ū. This usually imitates French usage in indicating [y]; the
OE value, [u], is then shown by *ou* or *ow* (also in the French
fashion). (Some speakers, however, probably substituted [ju]
for [y].)

ȳ. In ME this represents [i] and alternates freely with *i*; the
OE value, [y], is shown, as we have just seen, by *ū*.

ǣ, common in OE, ceased to be used in ME, in imitation of
French.

Short

a: [ɑ] or perhaps [a]; e.g., *hath* [haθ] or perhaps [haθ].

e: (1) [ɛ]; e.g., the first *e* in *helpe(n)*, 'to help', [ˈhɛlpə(n)];
(2) [ə]; e.g., the second *e* in *helpe(n)*, i.e., 'schwa'. This
latter sound occurs in unstressed syllables only, especially final
inflexional ones. OE uses the vowels *a, e, o* (occasionally), and
u in final inflexional syllables and, in EOE, they were doubtless
kept distinct in pronunciation, but in LOE they had all fallen
together into [ə], as unstressed vowels tend pretty generally to
do. That they did fall together is apparent from the confusion
of spelling in LOE mss, but the confusion was kept from becoming
complete by the persistence of some traditional conventions of
spelling. In EME, however, French writers, ignorant and careless
of traditional English orthography, usually spelt this schwa with
a single letter, viz., *e*, as was natural since that had become the
conventional way of writing the same sound in the same position

in French – a sound most often derived there from a final unstressed Latin -*am*.

i: [ɪ]; e.g., *s*(*c*)*hip*, 'ship', [ʃɪp].

o: (1) [ɒ]; e.g., *ofte*, 'oft', [ˈɒftə]; (2) [ʊ]; e.g., *sone*, 'son', [ˈsʊnə], OE *sunu*, [ˈsʊnu]. The usual ME substitution of *o* for the invariable *u* of OE in the first syllable of this word and in many others does not, at least in SEM, betoken a change in the sound – which remained the same, [ʊ] – but is a mere graphic device. In the handwriting of the ME period much more than in that of the OE, the letters *i* (and *j*), *u* (and *v*), *n*, *m*, and *w* tended to be made simply by one, two, or three short upright strokes (technically called minims) without horizontal connecting strokes at top or bottom between minims forming parts of the same letter, and sometimes without a dot over the single minim standing for *i* (or *j*). The result was that any word containing two or more of these letters in sequence became difficult to read, a succession of, say, four minims being interpretable as *nu, un, mi, wi, im, iw, ini, iui* (*ivi*), *nii, uii* (*vii*), *iin*, or *iiu* (*iiv*). In some contemporary French dialects, *o* had come, in certain phonetic situations, to indicate the same sound as *u*; and French scribes were not slow to substitute *o* very generally for *u* wherever *u* was etymologically called for in the neighbourhood of other letters made up of minims. This practice came to be widely imitated in writing English, and hence ME *sone*, which was easier to read than *sune*; and it persists in NE *son* and many other words, though there is less need for it in modern handwriting and hardly any in modern printing. With some exceptions, *o* was pronounced [ʊ] in ME where it is pronounced [ʌ] in the NE reflex, as it is in *son*.

u: (1) [ʊ]; e.g., *up* [ʊp]; (2) [y] (but less often than *ū* for [ȳ]).

y: [ɪ]; alternates freely with *i*, as *ȳ* does with *ī*; the OE value, [y], is shown by *u*, as we have just seen.

æ: like *ǣ*, not used in ME.

DIPHTHONGS (INCLUDING VOWEL DIGRAPHS)

ai, ay, ei, ey. These four digraphs are pretty much interchangeable. The first two always, and the second two usually, represent [aɪ], or perhaps rather [æɪ]. The second two – *ei* and *ey* – some-times, however, represent [e], depending on the etymology.

au: [aʊ]; e.g., *naught* [nɑʊxt].

ea: sometimes used for [ɛː], but much less frequent in ME spelling than in NE.

eu, ew: [ɪu] or [ɛu], depending on the etymology.

ie, ye: [i] or (less often) [e] (except as noted below), depending on the etymology.[1]

oa: sometimes used for [ɔ], but much less frequent in ME spelling than in NE.

oi, oy: [oɪ].

ou, ow: [u] or [ɒu], depending on the etymology.

Double vowels – especially *aa, ee, oo* – are used more or less systematically by some scribes to distinguish long sounds – [æː] (or [aː]), [ɛː] and [e], and [ɔ] and [o] – from short – [a] (or [a]), [ɛ], [ɒ].

The best way of putting all this to use is to look at a passage of ME along with a phonetic transcription. For this purpose we will use the best-known lines in ME – the opening sentence of the *Canterbury Tales*. But first we should heed several warnings, most of them to the effect that Chaucer's pronunciation may have been closer – as almost certainly the pronunciation of some of his acquaintances was closer – to NE than is indicated by the following very conservative transcription. Specifically, it is pos-sible (1) that, as has been said above, the long vowels were pronounced more nearly as they are in NE; (2) that in 'pro-nominal' words like *the, this, that, they, then, there, thus,* the earlier initial [θ] had already become (as in NE) [ð], when the words were unstressed, as they usually were and are; (3) that (again, in the normal unstressed use and position) the final sounds of *with,* of *of,* of *is* and *his,* and of *s*-plurals and genitive singulars whose ordinary singular forms ended in a voiced sound (e.g., *shoures,* line 1) were already voiced, as in NE; (4) that the endings *-es, -ed,* and *-eth* had the vowel [ə] rather than [ɪ]; (5) that (as has already been observed), stressed *u* in French

---

[1] *Ye,* when it stands by itself, can be confusing in that, when it means 'ye', 'you', it stands for [je] – i.e., *y* is there a consonant; but when it means 'eye', it stands for [iə] – i.e., *y* is there a vowel, and *e* indicates [ə].

words was already [ju] rather than [y]; (6) that the initial *h* of such words as *hath, have, his, hir, hem,* in their normal un-stressed position, was, as in NE, often slighted or even altogether dropped; (7) that short *a* may have been rather [a] than [ɑ]. Doubtless usage varied in these particulars among the people Chaucer daily conversed with in the London of the 1380s and 1390s; all we can say with confidence – but we *can* say it with confidence – is that the pronunciation indicated below would have been both intelligible to Chaucer and not altogether unfamiliar to him, though possibly a little old-fashioned or even 'back-country'.

Ever since 1933, it has been very properly customary, in quoting Chaucer, to use the admirable text of Professor F. N. Robinson's *The Complete Works of Geoffrey Chaucer,* Boston, etc., 1933; but the text printed below is, instead, that of J. M. Manly and Edith Rickert, *The Text of the Canterbury Tales,* Chicago, 1940, vol. 3, p. 3. This text is used here instead of Professor Robinson's not in any derogation of his as the now practically standard text, but rather partly because it is certainly closer (in punctuation or rather the lack of it, and capitalization and, probably, spelling) both to Chaucer's autograph and to the best scribal practice of his age and the age immediately succeeding, and partly in order to exemplify a ME text close to the best extant mss and illustrative of ME texts arrived at by the severest methods of recent scholarship. A phonetic transcription (subject to the warnings given above) is printed below.

> Whan that Aprill with his shoures soote
> The droghte of March hath perced to the roote
> And bathed euery veyne in swich licour
> Of which vertu engendred is the flour
> Whan Zephirus eek with his sweete breeth
> Inspired hath in euery holt and heeth
> The tendre croppes and the yonge sonne
> Hath in the Ram his half cours yronne
> And smale foweles maken melodye
> That slepen al the nyght with open eye
> So priketh hem nature in hir corages
> Than longen folk to goon on pilgrymages

And palmeres for to seken straunge strondes
To ferne halwes kouthe in sondry londes
And specially from euery shires ende
Of Engelond to Caunterbury they wende
The holy blisful martir for to seke
That hem hath holpen whan that they were seeke

[hwan θat ˈæː prɪl wɪθ hɪs ˈʃurɪs ˈsotə
θə druxt ɒf martʃ haθ ˈpersɪd to θə ˈrotə
and ˈbæː ðɪd ˈɛːv(ə)rɪ væin ɪn swɪtʃ lɪˈkur
ɒf hwɪtʃ vərˈty ɛnˈdʒɛndrɪd ɪs θə flur
hwan ˈzɛfɪrus ek wɪθ hɪs ˈswetə brɛː θ
ɪnˈspɪrɪd haθ ɪn ˈɛːv(ə)rɪ hɔlt and hɛː θ
θə ˈtɛndrə ˈkrɒpɪs and θə ˈjuŋgə ˈsunə
haθ ɪn θə ram hɪs half kurs ɪˈrunə
and ˈsmalə ˈfulɪs ˈmæː kn ˈmɛlo̩diə
θat ˈslepn̩ al θə nɪxt wɪθ ˈɔpn ˈiə
sɔ ˈprɪkɪθ hɛm naˈtyr ɪn hɪr kuˈræː dʒɪs
θan ˈlɒŋgn̩ fɒlk to gɔn ɒn ˈpɪlgrɪ̩mæː dʒɪs
and ˈpalmrs fɒr to ˈsekn̩ ˈstraundʒə ˈstrɒndɪs
to ˈfɛrnə ˈhalwɪs kuð ɪn ˈsundrɪ ˈlɒndɪs
and ˈspɛsjalɪ frɒm ˈɛːv(ə)rɪ ˈʃɪrɪs ˈɛndə
ɒf ˈɛŋgəlɒnd to ˈkauntr̩brɪ θæi ˈwɛndə
θə ˈhɒlɪ ˈblɪsful ˈmartr̩ fɒr to ˈsekə
θat hɛm haθ ˈhɒlpn̩ hwan θat θæi wɛr ˈsekə]

Two or three transcriptions here – e.g., [druxt] for *droghte*
(l. 2) and [ˈie] for *eye* (l. 10) – do not square with the list of
equivalences given above. This is not to say that the transcriptions are wrong but that the list of equivalences is in a few places
left deliberately incomplete in view of the elementary character
of this book.

Chapter XII

MIDDLE ENGLISH DIALECTS:
SCANDINAVIAN LOAN-WORDS

★

IN THE preceding chapter we have examined about as 'classical' a specimen as could be found of (L)ME – the opening lines of the greatest poem of the greatest ME writer, in the ME dialect that was already becoming, and eventually became completely, the standard dialect of NE, and in a text likely to resemble Chaucer's autograph more closely than any other that can ever be con- structed.[1] It may well serve as a point of departure into some discussion of ME dialects generally, especially those of the end of the fourteenth century and the beginning of the fifteenth, for which the available evidence is amplest.

In the first place, there *were* dialects in late-fourteenth-century English: by no means all Chaucer's contemporaries wrote (or spoke) as he did (though such was the prestige of London English coming to be that doubtless more of them wrote – nearly – as he did than spoke as he did). We know little about some ME dialects, even some late ones, but we know a great deal more about most of them than we do about most OE dialects. And we know enough about the dialects of both periods to say that most of the principal ME dialect boundaries were, by and large, about the same as the OE ones. Thus Northern ME occupied about the same territory as Northumbrian OE, Midland ME as Mercian OE, Southern (or better, South-western) ME as West Saxon OE, and

---

[1] The text now in general use – Robinson's – is fundamentally that of the Ellesmere ms produced within some ten years of Chaucer's death by an extraordinarily clear-headed, painstaking, methodical scribe. It gets its name, as many mss do, from a previous owner; specifically, from having been in the possession of several members of the Egerton family (succes- sively Lords Ellesmere) for some three centuries, until, in 1917, it was sold to the Huntington Library in California. In 1917, the expatriation may not have seemed 'a good idea'; in 1940, it did; in 1957, perhaps we have swung full circle.

Kentish ME (or better, South-eastern) as Kentish OE. There is, indeed, little reason for the existence of two nomenclatures except custom. But there are three important differences: (1) the ME descendant (Midland) of Mercian OE splits into two parts so different from each other that we may usefully distinguish them as West Midland (henceforth WM) and East Midland (EM); (2) the EM can often be almost as usefully divided into North EM (henceforth NEM) and SEM; and (3) we *do* make these distinctions because they are useful: we *can* make them because we have vastly more evidence than we have for OE. I.e., differences almost as clear and important perhaps occurred in OE, but we have too little OE writing left (apart from West Saxon) to be anywhere nearly as clear and sure as we can be about ME – at least LME.

The line between EM and WM is important. It can be imagined roughly as extending from about Lancaster south-eastward to a point about half-way between Sheffield and Derby, then south-ward to a point about half-way between Coventry and Oxford, and then south-westward to about Bristol. And the line between NEM and SEM is perhaps even more important: roughly speaking, the NEM territory comprised Lincs, most of Notts, the eastern part of Derbyshire, and the southern part of Yorks; the SEM territory comprised the rest of the more southerly (and con-siderably larger) part of the East Midlands.

It is of special importance that the SEM region included London (and Westminster), Oxford, and Cambridge: for if it had not, standard NE would be dialectally different from what it is. And as a kind of corrective to recent emphases, proper but perhaps a little overdone, we may well observe that it has certainly been important for at least the literary language that Chaucer (and Gower) wrote in the dialect of the South-east Midlands (speci-fically of London), though, to be sure, they did so mainly because they lived there.

The increasing difference among the dialects, and especially between EM and WM, indicates the degree to which, between *c.* 1100 and *c.* 1350, English was more or less (though increasingly less) submerged as a literary language, and the similar degree to which England, in part consequently, got along without a national standard of English: throughout its existence the language has reflected political and social and cultural history.

In many ways, to be sure, all ME dialects[1] show a common development. (1) They all replace OE spelling conventions with French ones, as we have seen. (2) All the scribes using any of the ME dialects replace OE handwriting with French, as we shall see in a little more detail later. (3) They all simplify OE inflexions.[2] (4) They all, partly in compensation, tend to use a more uniform and rigid word-order. (5) They all adopt many French and Latin words, both simple and compound. (6) They all construct new compound words out of native elements, but on French and Latin models and on an element-for-element basis – e.g., *notwithstanding*, imitating (Old) French *non obstant* or Latin *non obstante*. (7) They all imitate French and Latin

---

[1] This is probably the best place at which to give the warning that the determination of dialect names and boundaries (not only in ME but also in English generally, and not only in English but also in almost any language) is somewhat arbitrary and pragmatic. It is necessarily so. We must realize both that the principal ME dialects here named and characterized were not separated from each other by sharp lines and also that each dialect contained within itself a number of subdialects; and the southernmost Northern subdialects, e.g., blended into the northernmost Midland subdialects. A helpful analogy is to be found in the solar spectrum. That spectrum is actually an absolutely continuous belt with no sharp lines of division, but we find it practically useful – necessary, indeed – to think of it as made up of six or seven bands, shading into each other: for though we cannot say, of certain areas, whether they should be called yellow or green, certain other areas, again, are beyond question one or the other, and provide us with, so to speak, useful norms of reference.

[2] The most conspicuous and important instance of this simplification is the gradual spread of the ending *-es* [ɪs] or [əs] (or [ɪz] or [əz]) as the normal sign of both the genitive singular and the (especially nominative and accusative) plural of nouns. OE nouns of various declensions indicated these functions with various endings, all of which, in the same declensions or others, also indicated other functions. There were just two exceptions to this ambiguity: the ending *-as* (peculiar to the most numerous declension of masculine nouns) was never anything but the sign of the nominative and accusative plural, and *-es* never anything but the sign of the genitive singular (of the same masculine declension and also of the most numerous neuter declension). These uniquely unambiguous signs naturally recommended themselves above all others, whose place they gradually took in the very great majority of nouns in ME, whence the almost universal NE plural *-(e)s* and possessive (genitive) *-'s*.

idiom and syntax. (8) They all tend to reduce to [ə] all unstressed vowels, especially those in inflexional endings, and to spell this [ə] with *e*. (9) They all eliminate long or double consonants – in pronunciation, but not always in spelling. (10) They all lengthen short *a* (earlier often *æ*), *e*, and *o* – i.e., they make [ɑ] or [æ], [ɛ], and [ɒ] into, respectively, [ɑ:] (later [æ:]), [ɛ:], and [ɔ] – in open syllables.¹ Thus OE *bana* ['bɑnɑ], 'bane, murderer', becomes EME *bane* ['bɑ:nə], LME (SEM) ['bæ:nə]; OE *efen* ['ɛvɛn], 'even', ME *even* ['ɛ:vn]; and OE *ofer* ['ɒvɛr], 'over', ME *over* ['ɔvr].² (11) They agree, for the most part, in the 'values' of most consonant letters. (12) They all reduce the extremely common OE prefix *ge-* [jɛ], which is always unstressed, to *i-* or *y-* [ɪ], a syllable which, in LME or at least ENE, disappears almost without trace. Thus we read, in the opening sentence of the *Canterbury Tales*, about the sun's having 'yronne' his half course in one of the signs of the zodiac. 'Yronne' [ɪ'runə], NE 'run' (past participle), is here the reflex of OE *gerunnen* [jɛ'run-nɛn]; the NE *run* [rʌn] has, besides making [u] into [ʌ] and ceasing to pronounce (and spell) the final [ən], dropped the first syllable altogether. (13) They all tend to make OE [ɣ], in the neighbourhood of back vowels (in the neighbourhood of front ones it had already been replaced, in OE, by [j]), into [w] or [u].³ Thus OE *dagas*, 'days', ['dɑɣɑs], tends to

---

¹ An open syllable is usually defined, not very helpfully, as one ending in a vowel. Less simply but more illuminatingly and comprehensively, we may say that an open syllable is (1) a final one ending in a vowel, or (2) a non-final one whose vowel is separated from the vowel of the next syllable by only one consonant. E.g., in NE, (1) *beau* [bo] and (2) the first syllable of *boater* ['botə] are open syllables; *boat* [bot] and the first syllable of *boaster* ['bostə] (and for that matter *boast* [bost] by itself) are closed syllables.

² In various dialects at various times, but not generally or at any rate not for the most part permanently in fourteenth-century SEM, the other principal OE short vowels – [ɪ] and [u] – were also lengthened, but were in addition lowered, so that they became not [i] and [u], but [e] and [o]. A few standard NE pronunciations (and spellings), apparently importations into the London dialect, can probably be explained only in this way.

³ We cannot afford the space here to go into the precise circumstances in which OE [ɣ] is reflected, in ME, as [w], [u], or, in the final position, [x].

become ME *dawes* [ˈdɑwəs], whence the NE family name 'Dawes' [dɔz].[1] The NE plural of *day* would also historically be *daws [dɔz], but the increasing difference in sound (and also spelling) between LOE and EME singular [dæi] (or the like) and plural [ˈdɑwəs] eventually became, so to speak, too much to bear, with the result that the historical plural was abandoned in favour of a new analogical plural formed on the model of the historical singular, OE *dæg*, ME *day* [dæi] – *dayes* [ˈdæjəs] (or the like), whence NE *days* [dez]. It is not surprising that [ɣ], in the neighbourhood of back vowels, should tend to become [w] or [u]: [ɣ], like [w] and [u], is a high back sound; high back sounds – i.e., those in which the back of the tongue approaches the palate – tend, for anatomical reasons, to effect a rounding of the lips; and almost all that is needed to make [ɣ] into [w] or [u] is the gradually increasing 'emphasis' on the rounding

---

[1] The ways of English proper names, especially those of families and still more those of places, are fearful and wonderful, as most Englishmen know, both in pronunciation and in spelling. The spelling and pronunciation of other NE words are inconsistent and sometimes even mysterious, but comparatively they present a model of logic and system. Should we today tolerate, outside of proper names, such things as *Beauchamp* for [ˈbitʃm̩], or *Cholmondeley* for [ˈtʃʌmlɪ], or *M'*, *Mc*, *Mac*, and *Mack-*, all four, for [mək]? Would one ever guess that Cambridge was not named from the Cam, but that it was rather the other way round? – or that it all began with *Granta?* The explanation of this much greater difference between the sound and spelling of proper names than of other words is two-fold: (1) Each locality tends to develop its pronunciation of the whole language individually and divergently. This tendency is very much subject to inhibitions in words widely current in neighbouring localities, but place names, and family names more or less peculiar to the locality concerned, being less current outside, more or less escape such inhibitions. Thus such names tend to develop, unchecked, very various pronunciations in different districts. (2) At the same time, the *spellings* of these words tend to be, on the contrary, conservative, partly because they occur so often in more or less public documents – wills, deeds, charters, and the like – and partly because, especially in such documents, a sort of legalistic importance tends to become attached to preserving old spellings. The result of these two opposite movements is that place names, and to some extent family names, characteristically exhibit a greater difference between sound and spelling than the rest of the language does.

of the lips rather than on the high back position of the tongue. Here, as often, there is nothing exactly inevitable about the change, or even, strictly, predictable, but neither is there anything at all unnatural or surprising about it once it has taken place. In short, we cannot predict that one sound will develop into another, but we *can* predict that none will develop *immediately* into another produced in a radically different way.

Otherwise the dialects differ a good deal. Some of the most conspicuous differences are as follows: (1) Northern ME preserves OE *ā* [ɑː]; the other dialects 'back' it, raise it, and round it to [ɔ]: e.g., OE and Northern ME *hᵃm*, 'home', [hɑːm]; other ME dialects, *ho(o)m* [hɔm].¹ (2) West Midland ME preserves OE [Y] and [y] (spelt *y* and *ȳ* in OE, as in *hyll*, 'hill', and *fȳr*, 'fire'), but spells them *u*, and *ui* or *uy*, as in *hull* and *fuir* or *fuyr*;² most other dialects unrounded these vowels and accordingly spelt them *hill* and *fir* (or *hyll* and *fyr*), [hɪl] and [fir], though in Kentish they were often not only unrounded but also lowered to *hell* and *fer*, [hɛl] and [fer]. There is a good deal of dialect overlapping and mixture in Chaucer's time. Chaucer's own language, e.g., was SEM, to be sure, but SEM tinged with Kentish, so that Chaucer, though he usually said, e.g., *liste(n)* or *lyste(n)*, [ˈlɪstə(n)], from OE *lystan*, [ˈlystɑn], 'to please', felt free, when he needed a rhyme, to say *leste(n)*, in the Kentish fashion. Again, the third syllable of 'Canterbury' is now pronounced

¹ Note, incidentally, how this ME difference is reflected in NE, where we have Scots (descended from extreme Northern ME) *hame* [hem] and Southern (Standard) *home* [hom]; in ENE, (E)ME [ɑː] (everywhere) became ultimately (e), and [ɔ] became [o].

² The use of *i* or *y* merely to indicate a long preceding vowel (here [y], spelt *u*), and not as a sign of a sound in itself, is common (even usual) in the north, whence it seems to have worked its way into the West Midlands. It must have begun with *e(i)*. As we have seen, [e] tends to differ from [ɛ] (and [ɛː]) by attaching to itself a following [i], so that *ē* (as distinguished from *ę̄*) and *ei* may represent nearly the same sound. The result, especially among speakers of ME who did not use or readily hear the [i] after the [e] or [ɛ], was that *i* seemed to be a convenient way of showing a long preceding vowel – any vowel, not just *e*. In time, then, *ai*, *oi*, and *ui* (and *ay*, *oy*, and *uy*) came, among some scribes, particularly Northern ones, to be a common way of writing [ɑː], [o] or [ɔ], and [y] as distinguished from [ɑ], [ɒ], and [Y].

E

(when it is not merely syncopated, i.e., suppressed altogether)
as it historically should be in the Kentish district, viz., [ɛ], but
the spelling – *u,* after the French model – reflects rather the
Western ME [Y] inherited from OE without change. (3) Southern
ME generally voiced OE initial [f], [θ], and [s] to [v], [ð], and
[z] respectively (as indeed Southern OE may have done). Two
or three of these southern forms got into standard NE (probably
from Kentish, specifically) – e.g., *vat* and *vixen* (for normal
SEM **fat* and **fixen*), from OE *fæt* and *fyxen.*

There are other differences in sounds among ME dialects, but
we had better go on to a few differences in grammatical forms.
Everyone knows 'Scots wha hae wi' Wallace bled'; not everyone
(outside of Scotland) knows that it is very bad Scots (as Burns
did know, but he wanted English readers), and should be 'Scots
(th)at has'. Again, the great fourteenth-century prelate William
of Wykeham's motto, conveyed to his foundation, Winchester
School (not far from where he was born and learnt his English),
was 'Manners maketh man'. Now nothing could seem more
obvious, to most English-speaking people today, than that 'Scots
that has' and 'manners maketh' are ungrammatical, and should
be 'Scots that' (or 'who' or 'wha') 'have' (or 'hae', as indeed
Burns makes it), and 'manners make'. And yet they were respectively, in northern and south-western English, perfectly good
grammar. The fact is that 'has' and 'maketh' here, though
identical in form with standard NE singular verbs, are so accidentally, and are perfectly legitimate and historically regular
plural forms in their respective dialects. In West Saxon the
present plural indicative of almost all verbs ended in -þ, but,
in Northumbrian, often in -s, and this *s* spread and remained in
Northern ME, where it is reflected in *has* (plural). In Mercian,
also, the ending was in -þ, but in that dialect the subjunctive
ending, *-en,* came in the course of time to be much more commonly substituted for the indicative -(*i*)*aþ* than it was in West
Saxon. This *-en,* [ɛn] in OE, [ən] in EME, was commonly reduced
to [ə] in LME and ceased to be pronounced altogether in ENE,
though we still often preserve it in spelling (e.g., *make* [mek]).

Another difference, in grammatical form, between Northern
and non-Northern ME, noticeable until the sixteenth century, is
one in the case forms of the personal pronoun of the third person

plural. In OE these were normally *hīe* (nominative and accusative), *heom* (dative and instrumental), and *heora* (genitive). In Southern ME these were approximately preserved for a long time as (normally) *he* or *hi*, *him* or *hem*, and *her(e)* or *hir(e)*. But these developments posed some practical difficulties. *He* or *hi* was also the normal ME development of the OE *hē* (masculine nominative singular), *hēo* (feminine nominative singular), and *hīe* (feminine accusative singular – identical with the nominative and accusative plural already in OE); *him* or *hem*, of *him* (masculine and neuter dative and instrumental singular); and *her(e)* or *hir(e)*, of *hiere* (feminine dative, genitive, and instrumental singular); imagine how inconvenient it would be in NE if we had only one word to signify 'they', 'them', 'he', 'she', and 'her'.

Deliverance was found, at first in the North, by judicious imitation of, or rather borrowing from, the language of the Scandinavian settlers in England. These Scandinavians, speaking a language closely related to OE, had met earlier with the same kind of confusion, owing to the same cause, viz., changes in sound, and had solved the problem by coming gradually to substitute, for their cognates of the OE personal pronoun forms *hīe*, *heom*, and *heora*, their cognates of the OE demonstrative pronoun forms *þā*, *þǣm*, and *þāra*, cognates which were not confusable with the Scandinavian cognates of the OE singular forms *hē*, *hēo*, feminine accusative *hīe*, and *hiere*. Late northern Anglo-Saxons sensibly imitated their Scandinavian neighbours, or rather adopted their forms, which have eventuated in NE *they*, *them*, and *their*.[1]

Northern ME was quick to use all these forms. Midland – especially SEM – early adopted the nominative (NE *they*), but was slow to adopt also the rest, so that Chaucer writes in SEM *c.* 1390 that pilgrims travel from all over England to Canterbury 'the holy . . . martir for to seke/ That *hem* hath holpen whan that *they* were seke', and, a few lines earlier, that in the springtime Nature stimulates the birds 'in *hir* corages' ('hearts').

When a language goes to the almost unexampled length of supplanting such fundamental elements of its native vocabulary

---

[1] If the late northern Anglo-Saxons had used native OE forms instead of borrowing Scandinavian ones, we should probably now be saying **tho* [ðo], **thome* or **theme* [ðom] or [ðim], and **thore* [ðɔ(ə)].

as personal pronouns by borrowed ones, it would obviously be
very surprising if it did not also borrow other words from the
same source. We are not confronted here with any such surprise.
It is comparatively easy for any English-speaking person knowing something of French and Latin, and perhaps Greek, to go
through a ME or NE text and pick out the French and Latin (and
Greek) loan-words, but it is almost as easy for him to conclude
that the residue are all (at least in ME) native English. That
conclusion would be a mistake: many of them are Scandinavian.
Both the conclusion, and the fact that it would be a mistake, are
natural, for several reasons: (1) Most such words express very
common and familiar notions – so common and familiar that one
finds it hard to believe that the words have not always been a
part of the vocabulary. (2) Most of them look much more like
native words than they do like loan-words. This fact is owing
to two causes: (a) Scandinavian is much more closely and fundamentally related to English than French or Latin is; Scandinavian
words, therefore, will naturally resemble English ones more
closely – so closely, indeed, that it is not always possible to be
sure whether this or that ME word has survived from OE or been
imported from Scandinavian. (b) Most Scandinavian words were
borrowed by English before – long before – most Latin and
almost all French ones; and loan-words, once thoroughly incor-
porated into the language borrowing them, share in the general
phonetic and formal development of the native vocabulary. There
are two very remarkable facts about Scandinavian loan-words in
English, besides their great number and the common and familiar
quality of the meanings of many: (1) that, though most of them
must have made their way into the language from the ninth
century to the eleventh, they do not appear numerously in
extant records till the thirteenth; and (2) that they became
and remain very numerous even in regions not among those
most largely settled by Scandinavians, including much of the
SEM region. It would not be easy to think of a NE word that one
would more confidently expect to be native than *law;* and yet
it is not native, but Scandinavian. Again, most NE (and SEM ME)
words beginning with *sk* are Scandinavian, the reason being that
Germanic [sk] became OE [ʃ] – OE *sc,* ME *sh, ssh, sch,* etc., NE
sh – but remained [sk] – *sk* – in (early) Scandinavian, so that,

e.g., *skirt*, a Scandinavian loan-word, is the doublet of native English *shirt*. The late appearance, in literary records, of many Scandinavian loan-words that must have entered the everyday spoken language centuries earlier is evidence both of the long submergence of English as an important literary language and also of the growth of literary ME predominantly not out of literary OE, but out of colloquial, at least in vocabulary.

Chapter XIII

MIDDLE ENGLISH LITERATURE

★

ALL extant OE literature is contained in some forty volumes averaging, say, 300 pages about five inches by eight. Of these *c.* 12,000 pages, at least three-fourths are given to 'apparatus' – introductions, notes, glossaries. Computing 350 words to the page, all extant OE literature comprises just about a million words – not many more than are printed every Sunday (or rather Saturday afternoon) in the *New York Times*, and hardly as many as have been written by any of the hundreds of modern novelists who have published a dozen volumes apiece.

We have already seen that we have several reasons for believing that these million words are a very small part of the English literature produced up to the Norman Conquest or thereabout, and that they by no means necessarily or even probably give us a proportionally accurate and typical impression of what OE literature as a whole was, or even of what the best of it was. ME literature is in a different situation, for several reasons. The most obvious one – that the population was larger – is the least important, for the population was not, in point of fact, very much larger (it underwent, indeed, a sharp reduction about the middle of the fourteenth century, in consequence of the Black Death), and the potential English-reading public was in all probability actually smaller in the twelfth century than it had been in the eleventh (though it certainly became larger, and on the whole increasingly so, in the thirteenth, fourteenth, and fifteenth). The really important reasons why there is so much more ME literature (or rather writing) extant than OE – something like twenty times more – are (1) that no such cataclysmic interruption of literary and general cultural continuity has occurred between ME and NE as occurred, in the shape of the Norman Conquest, between OE and ME; (2) the simple fact that the ME period is later than the OE; and (3) the invention of printing (or rather of movable type),[1] which came at the very end of the ME period.

From surviving ME literature, therefore, we can obtain a much more extensive and balanced and nearly complete picture of the cultural life of the age than we can obtain of the OE period from surviving OE literature: many people have read all the OE literature extant, but none have read all the ME literature extant, if only because a good deal of it has never been printed (though almost all of it has been that is clearly worth printing and that is describable as 'literature' in the sense of *belles lettres*). And yet in many ways surviving ME literature resembles surviving OE literature more closely, in its relation to the society and culture of its time, than it does NE literature. The ME period, like the OE and unlike the NE, was one in which verse bulked large, even in the treatment of what seem to us essentially unpoetic subjects; in which comparatively little (though much more than in OE) was written – confessedly, at least – for sheer entertainment; in which few people, according to modern

---

[1] It is important to understand that the revolution – probably the most momentous revolution in the history of the world – commonly called the invention of printing is more accurately called the invention of movable type. 'Printing', in the proper sense of producing copies by *pressing* an inked 'type' – i.e., reversed model – on paper (or parchment or other receptive surface) is very old: it was a common means of producing copies of wood-cuts – first of drawings but later of written words – very early among the Chinese and much later, but still well before the invention of movable type, among the Europeans. The commonness and cheapness of books today result not from 'printing' but rather from the contrivance of *movable* (and hence *re-usable*) *metal types of single letters*. The 'invention of printing' consisted essentially in discovering that, appearances and expectations however much to the contrary, it is in the long run much more expeditious and hence cheaper to print pages by 'setting up' single-letter but re-usable types of metal than it is either to print them from whole-page engraved blocks or to reproduce them one by one through the instrumentality of scribes. The 'invention of printing', as it is commonly called, consists essentially in overcoming the (very considerable) technological difficulties involved, as, indeed, most 'inventions' do: Roger Bacon in the thirteenth century perfectly understood the theory of the microscope and the telescope, but he could never have produced either, because contemporary technology was not equal to constructing them.

standards, habitually read at all; in which much of the literary
production was in other languages (Latin as in the OE period,
but now French also) than the vernacular; in which most
popular 'literature' was still not written at all, but recited orally,
or, if written, was still designed primarily or exclusively for
oral recitation; and in which religious themes and didactic purpose were still much more common than they are today.

A number of these points and several others, which, like them,
illustrate certain important differences between NE literature and
ME (and sometimes OE), deserve some further remarks, especially
because the differences are precisely those of which ignorance
will perplex or mislead or repel the modern reader. And first,
the mediaeval attitude toward antiquity, especially classical
antiquity.

The middle ages, generally speaking, held toward classical
antiquity an attitude that seems to the modern mind inconsistent,
or, to use a favourite modern word, ambivalent. Mediaeval
people venerated classical antiquity for its obvious intellectual,
artistic, and cultural superiority, but simultaneously – or perhaps, to be Freudian, we might say 'consequently' – pitied it
and even scorned it because it lacked 'the one thing needful', the
Christian faith. Today we are not made uncomfortable by feeling
obliged to admire this or that aspect of classical antiquity and
at the same time to scorn and reject that or this: we trust, i.e.,
a good deal more in the essential and eternal rightness and
wholeness of our own standards and point of view than the
middle ages did in the essential rightness and wholeness of theirs.
In the middle ages – oddly enough, if we think of them as the
'age of faith' – a sort of scared respect for ancient art and wisdom
dominated over pity and contempt for ancient infidelity and
blindness. St Thomas Aquinas Christianized Aristotle, to be
sure, but he thought him eminently worth Christianizing: and
Dante does not venture to assign to the ancient worthies a less
easy room in hell than one which to the modern mind seems
far easier than a stall, however comfortably *miserere*'d, in the
celestial choir eternally hymning the glory of God in Paradise,
meanwhile squinting at the Beatific Vision. Better fifty years
of Plato than a cycle of Bernard: how much better still a cycle
of Plato!

A striking illustration of this veneration for classical antiquity is to be found in one of the greatest of English poems, Chaucer's *Troilus and Criseyde* (*c.* 1387). Chaucer's source was Boccaccio's *Il Filostrato* ('the victim of love'), a poem composed in Italian some forty years earlier. Chaucer may not have known Boccaccio's name, but he certainly knew he was adapting a *modern Italian* poem; and yet he claims to be following an *ancient Latin* one by a certain 'Lollius', and goes to the length, in his mystification, of turning Boccaccio's Italian names *Troilo* and *Pandaro* into the Latin 'Troilus' and 'Pandarus'. He frequently refers, furthermore, to 'Lollius' as his 'auctor'. Now the NE of *auctor* is 'author', i.e., '(original) writer'; but *auctor* had for the middle ages a much more exclusive sense than NE 'author'; it ordinarily meant '(classical) *authority*' – i.e., (ancient and classical) source of original and *authentic*[1] information. Thus when Chaucer talks about his *'auctor* called Lollius', he means much more than a modern translator would mean, viz., 'the *writer* whose work I am translating from his language into mine': he means (or rather pretends to mean) 'the ancient and classic and therefore great and venerable (and incidentally pre-Christian and therefore pagan) *authority* on whom I depend'. Again, one of the 'authors' whom Chaucer used to supplement Boccaccio's treatment of the story of Troilus and Cressida was the twelfth-century English Joseph of Exeter, whose Latin poem *De Bello Trojano* was frequently regarded, in the later middle ages, as the *De Excidio Trojae*, probably written in the sixth century, but

---

[1] The NE spelling of *author* and the ME meaning of the word, reflected in the NE meaning of the related *authority* and *authoritative*, suggest a relation to the word *authentic*. The relation is non-existent. *Author* is a Latin word (*auctor*) meaning 'augmenter', 'increaser', 'promoter', and hence 'originator' (especially of a literary work): *authentic* is a Greek one meaning 'personally responsible', 'governing'. The middle ages tended to confuse or at least to associate the two (e.g., Dante, *Convivio*, fourth treatise, chapter six) and recorded that confusion or association, with a characteristic happy ignorance of etymology, by introducing *th* (the Latin transliteration of Greek θ) into the spelling of the Latin *auctor*, which became, often, *au(c)thor* – whence NE *author*. This bad spelling has affected the NE pronunciation, which ought to be [ˈɔtə], as *Thomas* is [ˈtɔməs] and *Thames* [tɛmz], but which has become [ˈɔθə].

commonly thought, in the middle ages, to have been composed
by one Dares Phrygius, an alleged participant in the Trojan
War. The middle ages wanted their 'authorities' as ancient and
'authoritative' as they could get them. Yet again, the middle
ages, being hungry for what they regarded as authentic information about classical antiquity, were more inclined than we are to
value classical writers for their supposed information rather than
for their art. 'Vergil', mediaeval men said to themselves, 'tells us
a lot; he was a great poet; so do Lucan and Statius; therefore so
were they.' The result was that in the middle ages Lucan and
Statius had nearly as great a reputation as Vergil.

This modest respect for classical predecessors is easily extended
to predecessors whether classical or not: the typical mediaeval
writer's boast was not so likely to be 'I have done what none
has done before' as 'I have done in some way perhaps better
what many have done before'. 'Originality', in the full modern
sense, almost vanishes from much even of so great a work as
the General Prologue of the *Canterbury Tales* in the light of the
Roman de la Rose[1] – vanishes so far, indeed, that we should now
regard Chaucer as a plagiarist. But the middle ages had very
different conceptions of plagiarism from ours, partly because of
the anonymity of much literature produced or at least circulating
then, partly because of mediaeval men's ingrained modesty in
the face of their fathers' accomplishments, and partly because
of their strong sense of 'social responsibility' – of the overriding

---

[1] The *Roman de la Rose*'s claims to being the most important vernacular
literary work of the middle ages can hardly be contested except by the
Divine Comedy – which indeed could contest them at all only in respect of
its influence since the later middle ages, not during them. The first 4,000
lines of the *Roman* were composed *c.* 1240 by Guillaume de Lorris in the
sentimental but worldly vein of courtly love; the remaining 16,000 lines
c. 1280 by Jean (Clopinel or Chopinel) de Meun(g), at least equally
worldly but infinitely less sentimental – the Voltaire, indeed, of the
thirteenth century, and a salutary corrective to oversimplified notions of
the middle ages as the age either of faith or of amorous sentimentality.
The collocation of the two writers is astonishing: it is somewhat as if
Pamela had been left incomplete by Richardson and pieced out by Fielding.
The poem was the chief furniture of Chaucer's mind, whether or not
Chaucer produced any or all of the extant ME (partial) translation.

obligation to edify and instruct, and even to entertain, as many men as possible with the best reading matter possible.

At the same time that the middle ages stood in awe of classical antiquity, they felt what may seem to us a paradoxical sense of continuity and identity with it – a sense perhaps growing out of a sense of sympathy and fellowship. This 'interaeval' feeling leads often to what will strike us as anachronisms (thus ancient Jewish and even Trojan high priests are called 'bishops', heathen temples 'churches', and ancient warriors 'knights'), and, among comparatively ignorant writers, produces an engaging fore-shortening of chronology, reminiscent of a speech put by Thomas Hardy into the mouth of one of his nineteenth-century Wessex rustics: ' "Casterbridge is an old, hoary place o' wickedness, by all account. 'T is recorded in history that we rebelled against the King one or two hundred years ago, in the time of the Romans, and that lots of us was hanged on Gallows Hill, and quartered, and our different j'ints sent about the country like butcher's meat; and for my part I can well believe it." '

The continuity between OE and ME literature is on the whole decidedly slight. Professor R. W. Chambers has indeed shown that ME and NE expository (and especially homiletic) prose owes much to a tradition continuous from OE times;[1] and the amazing though short-lived efflorescence of alliterative verse in the fourteenth century, after a long night, betokens unmistakably a persistence of the technique in popular oral tradition and of an appreciative audience for it: we need only instance the uniquely wonderful poem *Piers Plowman* (c. 1370) and its use of an alliterative system of versification (and one without rhyme) essentially identical with that of *Beowulf*.

The long night of native alliterative verse was not, indeed, completely dark: slight but almost continuous gleams are visible from the tenth century (and, of course, earlier) to the fourteenth: but despite that fact, and despite the occasional attempts at combining alliteration with rhyming and syllable-counting verse

---

[1] See his introduction on 'The Continuity of English Prose from Alfred to More and His School' in *The Life and Death of Sir Thomas Moore* [*sic*], etc., ed. E. V. Hitchcock, Early English Text Society, Original Series ‡ ‡ 186, London, 1932. Also published separately.

in, e.g., Layamon's[1] *Brut* (*c.* 1200) and the very great West-Midland poems of Chaucer's time, *Pearl* and *Sir Gawain and the Green Knight*, the native Germanic alliterative system was not destined to become the dominant form of English verse.

This position was reserved for rhymed and syllable-counting forms imitated from French. These were the forms exclusively used by Chaucer and Gower in the latter half of the fourteenth century, and all but exclusively by their successors among English poets ever since. That Chaucer was admired and imitated can surprise no one; that Gower was almost equally so for at least a century after his death must surprise a generation of whom many hardly know his name. And yet Gower, though greatly Chaucer's inferior as a poet, was an almost equally expert and resourceful versifier, a skilful teller of entertaining tales, and, much more than Chaucer, a citizen, a member of society, decidedly and even perhaps excessively aware of his supposed duty to his fellows. He is, furthermore, almost the only member of Chaucer's generation strictly comparable to him in being a very productive writer of polished English verse in the French manner. It is hardly an exaggeration to call Chaucer and Gower French poets writing in English. Gower, indeed, did not entrust his fame to English: he wrote some 35,000 lines of English verse, but also almost as many in French and about a third as many in Latin. Likewise, though Chaucer himself wrote, so far as we know, only in English, Englishmen even as late as the seventeenth century could still be so uncertain of the permanence of English as a literary language that Bacon, as is well known, put some of his English writings into Latin, and that, in the 1630s, Sir Francis Kinaston did the same for both Chaucer's *Troilus and Criseyde* and Robert Henryson's sequel to it, *The Testament of Cresseid*. Reverting again to Chaucer's time, we may note that Wyclif published both an English and a Latin

---

[1] The spelling here used – 'Layamon' – has led to a spelling pronunciation [ˈlejəmən] or [ˈlɑjəmən] which is probably too well established to be supplanted, but which is none the less based on a mistakenly generalized equation of ME ȝ ('yogh') with NE *y*. ME ȝ between back vowels regularly becomes NE *w*, and the second syllable of *Laȝamon* would regularly disappear, so that the proper NE form of the name would be 'Lawman'.

version of several of his polemical works, with a view to winning, through the Latin more certainly than through the English, the hearing not only of his learned contemporaries but also of posterity. Vernacular literature generally, in the middle ages, tended to be regarded with such contempt, or at least condescension, that it hardly even began to become a subject of serious critical study before the seventeenth century : it is astonishing that Chaucer wrote so much English poetry as he did and that he lavished such pains on it, especially considering that he gives almost no evidence of knowing any earlier English literature for which he can have had any respect. When he does acknowledge the existence of contemporary or earlier English literature, he does so mainly only in order to sneer at it, as he does in 'The Tale of Sir Thopas', a severe – and just – satire on the degenerate romances mass-produced for the rising middle classes (from which Chaucer's own family, incidentally, had sprung). This is not to say that English literature still admirable and still admired was not being produced outside of Chaucer's very narrow courtly Westminster circle. We must always remember that great and maddening poem *Piers Plowman*, and we should not forget at least two contemporary poems produced at the same time in the wilds of Cheshire or Lancashire – greatly superior to *Piers Plowman*, and equal to Chaucer, in literary polish and finesse and sophistication – *Sir Gawain and the Green Knight* and *Pearl*, the latter of which, at least, would probably, in its unashamed other-worldliness and sustained elevation, have abashed and disconcerted Chaucer – who, such was the difference in dialect, could hardly have read it with much understanding. We have not the slightest notion of who wrote *Pearl* and *Sir Gawain*, or even of whether a single man wrote both, and they were not destined, as Chaucer's poetry was (and Gower's), to supply the models of the English literature of the future, even as much as *Piers Plowman* was. They are not, therefore, essential reading for a modern interested in knowing only the English literature that belongs clearly to the main stream; but not to have read *Pearl* is to be the poorer.

Though *Pearl* and *Sir Gawain* may be called provincial and literally 'eccentric' in using, in one degree or another, the more or less insular and retrogressive alliterative form and also in

using a 'back-country' dialect, they are fully abreast of the times
in the knowledge their author or authors show of the contemporary or nearly contemporary language, literature, and
culture of France. English literature of the fourteenth century
imitated often, commonly, and closely almost every contemporary
French *genre* and form. There is only one conspicuous exception:
outside of the *Canterbury Tales*, surviving ME literature contains only two or three *fabliaux*. The *fabliau* was a short story
in verse, almost always humorous, very often satirical, and
characteristically more or less bawdy; more concerned with plot
than with character; and typically dealing with (and perhaps
chiefly appealing to) the urban middle or lower-middle classes.
Some 150 French *fabliaux* survive from the twelfth, thirteenth,
and early fourteenth centuries, many more must have been composed, and some give evidence of having been derived from
English originals: and yet of English *fabliaux* we have hardly a
twentieth as many, and three-fourths of these are Chaucer's.
One is driven to suppose that a sort of pre-Victorian Victorianism
in mediaeval England largely confined the smoking-car story
to oral tradition.

Oral tradition, however that may be, was incomparably more
important in the middle ages than it is today, not so much
because fewer people could read even their vernacular (though
certainly fewer could) as because books were so much rarer and
dearer: fewer people could and yet fewer did commonly bother
to read because, if for no other reason, they could not afford to
buy copies of such reading matter as there was.[1] That does not
mean that they had no appetite for literary amusement and
instruction; but it does mean that most people had to satisfy that
appetite for the most part by being read to rather than by

[1] Some notion of the costliness of books may be obtained from a letter
of *c.* 1380, quoted from *The Stonor Letters and Papers*, 1290–1483, by
Edith Rickert in *Chaucer's World*, edd. C. C. Olson and M. M. Crow,
Columbia University Press, N.Y., 1948, p. 116. A chaplain who has visited
a Stonor boy at his boarding school reports to the boy's father that the
boy must have what we should call a textbook, or rather a collection of
textbooks in one volume, that will sell for twelve shillings. Twelve shillings
at the end of the fourteenth century was the equivalent of something like
£25 today! And the chaplain thought it a very reasonable price.

reading. Consequently – inevitably – a class of professional public readers or reciters (roughly speaking, 'minstrels') is a fixed and prominent element of society up to the sixteenth century when the growing cheapness of (printed) books began bringing about their gradual decline. These *diseurs*, who must have been for the most part itinerant, naturally acquired, from constant repetition of their repertory, one degree or another of transfer of dependence from their mss to their memories. This transfer had several important results: (1) The *diseurs* often wrote down, from memory, their repertories for the use of their apprentices, and, human memory and understanding and taste being always fallible, tended to introduce endless corruptions, adaptations,[1] and other variations into literary texts;[2] (2) texts often preserve plain

[1] Sometimes allusive, not to say toad-eating, and also often pernicious to rhythm; one is now and then reminded of Silas Wegg:

> *Beside that cottage door, Mr Boffin,*
>   *A girl was on her knees;*
> *She held aloft a snowy scarf, Sir,*
>   *Which (my elder brother noticed) fluttered in the breeze.*

The parallel is by no means far-fetched; Mr Boffin furnished exactly the kind of audience the mediaeval minstrel was used to.

[2] What is certainly a very remarkable instance – if it is an instance at all – of the extent to which such modifications could be carried is to be found according to Professor Aage Brusendorff, *The Chaucer Tradition*, London and Copenhagen, 1925, in the ME (partial) translation of the *Roman de la Rose*. This translation, long attributed to Chaucer, falls into three sections, of which the first displays a usage very like Chaucer's, the third a usage somewhat less like his, and the second a usage very different from his – so different, indeed, that, if the fragment is really Chaucer's in origin, it has certainly been profoundly altered. Professor Brusendorff believed that such an alteration, through a *diseur*'s efforts to make good the deficiencies of his memory, was on the whole more likely than what seems to be the only alternative – the assumption that the late fourteenth century saw two or even three partial English translations of the *Roman*, as would seem rather unlikely, especially considering that we have independent evidence for only one, viz., Chaucer's. The thesis is hardly subject to proof, and raises, perhaps, as many difficulties as it clears away; but one must admit that it acquires a certain relative plausibility when one considers the conditions of mediaeval literary recitation and the astounding differences between extant texts of certain other mediaeval literary works.

signs of the conditions of oral recitation: thus such popular romances as *King Horn* and *Havelok* (both of the thirteenth century), and such a satire on such romances as Chaucer's 'Tale of Sir Thopas' (in the *Canterbury Tales*), regularly begin each section with appeals for the attention of the audience, as does even so sophisticated and upper-class a contemporary document as *Troilus and Criseyde*.

No modern can examine ME literature (or OE) without being impressed, and perhaps depressed, by what is certain to seem to his mind an undue predominance of religious themes and concerns. In some ways this impression is exaggerated. In the first place, the conditions of mediaeval publication and even of life generally led inevitably to the multiplication and preservation of religious and other edifying works in a degree out of proportion, probably, with their actual production and popularity. In the second place, much mediaeval literature that we are likely to think of as religious is merely moralistic, and moralistic in an at least not peculiarly Christian or even religious way. 'Conduct' was 'three-fourths of life' for the middle ages as well as for Matthew Arnold, books were almost ruinously expensive to produce, and the popular appetite for literary entertainment was, as we have seen, in large measure satisfied by recitations: to use time and skill and parchment in recording a literary work – especially a vernacular one, which was, furthermore, as being vernacular, likely to be despised as ephemeral and nugatory – was an enterprise not to be entered upon lightly. In the third place, not only is much mediaeval literature, roughly and generally classifiable as 'religious', called more specifically and accurately, as we have seen, 'moralistic', but also much of it is still better called 'ecclesiastical': 'religion', to be sure, bulked larger in the middle ages than it does today, but the Church bulked larger still, and was by no means so nearly confined to what we should call strictly 'religious' concerns as it is today. Today the state is uniquely *the* inescapable and coercive form of social organization; in the middle ages, on the contrary, the Church came much closer to occupying that position. Inevitably, then, mediaeval literature is shaped and coloured by the great and overriding fact of the existence of the Church as an institution, even apart from religion and morality.

Of the many very long ME works that can be called 'religious' in the broad sense, most are either retellings of the Christian mythos, or confessional manuals. Those of the first sort contain usually not only the substance of the narrative parts of the Old Testament and the New, but also much secondary matter derived chiefly from apocryphal or rather pseudepigraphical sources, both pre-Christian Jewish and early Christian – imaginative expansions, so to speak, of the Old and New Testaments – 'corroborative detail, intended to give artistic verisimilitude to an otherwise bald and unconvincing narrative'. Many of these supplementary details were at least familiar to the mediaeval mind, and taken by it quite as seriously, as the substance of the canonical Scriptures – notably, e.g., the story of the fall of the angels (attached to the Old Testament) and that of the infancy of Christ (attached to the New); and these tales are reflected not only in the Latin and vernacular literature of the middle ages but also – signifying a popular mediaeval familiarity with the Christian (including the biblical) legend surpassing that of the age of the Protestant Reformation probably and that of the present day certainly – in sculpture, glass, wall painting, and ms miniatures. A sort of sub-class of these para-historical writings consists in collections of popular accounts of saints' lives, with a heavy accent on their miracles: accounts usually designed, it would seem, for oral recitation, or at least excerption, by the multitude of none too learned parish priests in their Sunday and saint's-day sermons. Such priests were also probably the chief immediate users of the second main class of long religious works in ME, viz., confessional manuals, containing minutely detailed definitions and exemplifications of the seven deadly sins. Such manuals sometimes carry the mediaeval passion for orderly and systematic schematization to excessive and even absurd lengths: and yet the modern age owes them a debt for their habituation of men's minds to the essentially scientific practice of thoughtful classification.[1]

[1] This is not to say that these 'guides for the guides of the people' were not sometimes instances of the blind leading the blind (who were expected to lead the yet blinder). Thus the Kentish monk Dan Michel of Northgate, writing in his *The Ayenbite of Inwit* (i.e., 'remorse of conscience' – note the element-for-element translation: *ayen-* is *re-*, *-bite* is *-morse*, *in-* is *con-*,

F

One thing that must strike any modern reader as odd about ME literature is the habitual employment of verse for many subjects that no one would nowadays think of treating except in prose. Some of the confessional manuals just mentioned are one instance; another is the many treatises and occasional poems of the fourteenth century on historical, political, and even economic and scientific subjects. This excessive and inappropriate or at any rate undiscriminating preference of verse to prose is owing to a complex of causes – the very early, traditional, and remarkably persistent association of verse with the higher concerns of life, and of prose with everyday business; the correspondingly earlier development, in almost all cultures, of verse than of prose as the normal form of 'literature'; and the much greater ease – very important in illiterate or semi-literate ages – of memorizing verse. When a mediaeval man with ideas – ideas of almost any kind – set up for author, he was almost as much more likely to write in verse rather than in prose as his modern successor is likely to do the opposite. Hence the essentially and even repellently unpoetic quality of much ME verse.

A final important difference between ME and NE literature is that far more ME literature was anonymous. Anonymity in modern literature is rare and getting rarer. It is getting rarer

and -*wit* is -*science*) in 1340, renders the first half of the second verse of the ninety-fourth Psalm (the ninety-fifth in the Authorized Version and the Book of Common Prayer) – 'Praeoccupemus faciem ejus [i.e., Domini] in confessione' – as 'Do we to worke Godes nebsseft ine ssrifte', i.e., 'Let us make God's countenance operate in confession'. This is not only grotesque, it is senseless. (The reading of the Authorized Version and the Book of Common Prayer – 'Let us come before his presence with thanksgiving' – brings out the meaning of the original Hebrew and is confirmed by the revised Vulgate Psalter of 1945 – 'Accedamus in conspectum ejus cum laudibus'.) But Dan Michel was convinced that 'preoccupy' meant 'preoccupy', and 'confession' 'confession', in the senses he was used to; and the Bible was the Bible; and who was *he* to know better? Some measure of the decline in literacy and critical sense between OE vernacular literature and ME may be found by comparing, with Dan Michel's translation of this phrase, that of Ælfric in his homily on St Gregory the Great, of some 350 years earlier: 'Uton forhradian Godes ansyne on andetnysse', says Ælfric – i.e., 'Let us anticipate God's presence by confessing [our sins]' – which, though mistaken, at least makes sense. Progress is not inevitable.

mainly because of vanity and the profit motive; but it was rarer even in the ENE period than in the ME, chiefly because of the invention of printing (or rather of movable type). ME writers, and mediaeval writers in general, attached their names to their autograph mss almost as commonly and determinedly as writers do today, but with pathetically less common and permanent effect, for accidental and mechanical and technological reasons that we shall look into in the following chapter. And yet they attached their names to their works only *almost* as commonly and determinedly, not quite; and, what is more important, their contemporaries and successors tended to be much more careless of preserving the attribution of literary works than we are today. One reason for this is that earlier ages than ours placed more value than we do on the social utility of a literary work and less on its potentialities for enhancing the reputation (or the income)[1] of the writer; another is that much ME literature – much of the best of it, aesthetically speaking – consists in short and scattered and fugitive lyric poems meant for the delectation of only the writer and sometimes a narrow circle of friends – never or seldom copied or widely circulated and not meant to be: far fewer writers in the middle ages than today, when they had said well something worth saying, thought it imperative, or would have thought it so even if it had been possible, to secure circulation, fame, copyright (which was not dreamt of), income (and income tax) in the uttermost parts of the earth or even in the next county.

Many ME lyrics (almost all anonymous) of a more or less artistic kind are preserved, and so are many popular ballads – or at least so are many ENE texts of many ME popular ballads – of a decidedly less artistic kind. But of what may be called the ME equivalent of Tin-Pan Alley songs – like the Tin-Pan Alley product, mostly what D. H. Lawrence called 'permissible pornography' – we have little but a first line here and there, as in 'My love is faren in londe' (i.e., 'my girl's gone to the country') and 'Com hider, love, to me' – both recorded by Chaucer in the *Canterbury Tales* ('The Nun's Priest's Tale' and the General

---

[1] Indeed, the professional writer – one who depends for his living chiefly on the circulation and sale of his writings – is hardly heard of before the sixteenth century.

Prologue respectively). And neither this anonymity nor its accompanying narrowness of fame is an accident of later ages: one of the half-dozen extant 'major fifteenth-century ms anthologies of ME secular lyrics', to quote Professor R. H. Robbins,[1] is made up, to the extent of at least three-fifths of its contents, of poems by Chaucer, Gower, Lydgate, and Hoccleve (or Occleve),[2] who were almost the only fourteenth- and early-fifteenth-century English poets (at least in the fashionable French vein) widely known in the fifteenth century: 'almost the only' to such an extent that a good many of the poems attributed to them by the Findern book are falsely attributed. In short, the period round about 1400 in England has left us many poems – often good poems – by many writers, but few of those writers' names have come down to us, hardly more were widely known in their own day, and the productions of many tended to be ascribed to the few writers that were widely known and esteemed.

The tendency to ascribe to a namable and esteemed writer, or even to a *single* writer *not* namable, is almost irresistible, and the more so the fewer writers we can name or identify: 'William Langland' – of whom we do not really know so much as that he existed – is credited with (virtually) the whole of each of the three versions of *Piers Plowman* – which, however, may have been the work of at least three principal writers, none of them necessarily named Langland or even William; *Pearl*, *Sir Gawain and the Green Knight*, and two other West-Midland poems are commonly assigned to a single author (called by the question-begging names 'the *Pearl*-poet' and 'the *Gawain*-poet') chiefly because the unique texts of all four occur in a single ms; and numbers of poems that Chaucer could not possibly have written were none the less confidently printed as his in the sixteenth century, and were not expelled from the canon till the end of the eighteenth century or even, some of them, till late in the nineteenth.[3]

---

[1] 'The Findern Anthology', *Publications of the Modern Language Association of America* 69.160ff. (1954).

[2] The latter two both lived from *c*. 1370 to *c*. 1450 and were both admirers and imitators of Chaucer.

[3] This sort of thing is ancient and universal. David traditionally composed psalms, and Solomon, proverbs; therefore any psalm is David's and any proverb Solomon's.

Chapter XIV

MEDIAEVAL PUBLICATION

★

No one can read much ME or other mediaeval literature, either vernacular or Latin, without being struck by the pervasive expression of a thirst for fame, especially literary fame, and of an accompanying melancholy resignation to the unlikelihood of securing it. The reason is partly the somewhat paradoxical fact, noted in the preceding chapter, that many writers, especially occasional and non-professional writers who produced little, had no hope whatever of fame and apparently little desire for it, but partly also three other things: (1) the mediaeval writer's frequent sense that the instruction and edification of the reading (or hearing) public were more important than his own reputation or that of any other individual, (2) the consequent carelessness of whether he appropriated or adapted an earlier writer's work but almost equally whether yet later writers appropriated or adapted his, and (3) the conditions of mediaeval publication, several of which combined to facilitate depriving a writer of credit for his writings. These conditions had at least two important effects: (1) Altogether false attributions were often made of works – even some of considerable length – whose true authors' names had been lost (e.g., the drearily protracted fourteenth-century theological 'poem' *The Pricke of Conscience*, long but quite wrongly assigned to the mystical writer Richard Rolle of Hampole – *ob.* 1348 – and sometimes, alternatively (in the late middle ages if not in modern times), to Bishop Robert Grosseteste of Lincoln – *ob.* 1253 (!)).[1] (2) Mediaeval works tend

---

[1] On the falsity of the attribution of *The Pricke of Conscience* to Rolle, see H. E. Allen, *Writings Ascribed to Richard Rolle*, etc., London, 1927. Note also – considering that Grosseteste flourished a whole century earlier than either Rolle or the manifest period of the poem – how little sense of the changes in the English language was possessed by late mediaeval scribes: and yet they should not be blamed very severely, considering that they quite naturally had no expectation that their exemplars would display

to be added to by later writers, often without declaration. We have already glanced at an example of this sort of accretion *with* declaration in the *Roman de la Rose*, and at a *possible* example of it without declaration in *Piers Plowman*; and so common was this passing off (intentional or unintentional) of the work of two or more writers as the work of one that some wit has drily generalized that 'all mediaeval literature is the work of three men – A, B, and an interpolator.'

It has been observed above that much of this anonymity, pseudonymity, and accretion and other modification was owing to the conditions of mediaeval publication. This statement inevitably raises the question, 'How can we properly speak of "publication" before the age of printing?'

The answer is, 'Very easily and very properly.' Publication essentially consists, after all, not in the *printed* multiplication of a literary work, but in its (at least potential) *multiplication* (and general availability), simply and generally. A mediaeval writer, when he 'published' at all, did so, most commonly, by presenting a fair copy of his work to his patron (if he had one), or by allowing his friends or their agents to reproduce it, or by giving over his autograph to the masters of commercial *scriptoria* (which indeed existed, and which were the 'ancestors' and models of modern printing offices and publishing houses). In none of these situations was there anything like 'copyright', but in all three of them, or at least in the second and third, some degree of multiplication was made probable or certain, as well as some degree of fidelity and accuracy. The object, i.e., in either the second situation or the third, was to supply both more or less numerous and (secondarily) faithful reproductions of the original. But there is one essential difference between a ms text – even a commercially produced one – and any given copy of a printed text, viz., that the function of a scribe in copying a ms is essentially just like that of a compositor in setting up a printed text, so that any ms is comparable rather to a single but whole printing of a work than to an individual instance of that printing. It follows that, if we have however many 'copies' (i.e., individual

clearly the dialectal traits, either temporal or geographical, of the original work, and had themselves, furthermore, a much less exact idea of those traits than we have.

instances) of a single printing together with a single ms (and another than that from which the printer worked), then the single ms affords by itself, other things being equal, just as valid and independent evidence of what the writer wrote as all the printed copies together, however numerous.[1]

'What the writer wrote' is as a rule much harder to discover from the mss or early printed editions of mediaeval works than it is from the printed editions of a modern one. A number of reasons account for this. (1) The multitude of (sometimes ambiguous and misleading) abbreviations in use in OE increased in ME. (2) Handwriting tended to become less legible in the later middle ages, though by no means usually less beautiful; indeed, the elaboration of ornament and mannerism rather tended to reduce legibility. (3) The variety of dialect and spelling often led to misunderstanding and hence miscopying, which was often perpetuated in later copies of copies. (4) Most scribes paid little heed to reproducing exactly the spelling and grammatical forms of their exemplars even when they understood them. (5) Scribes often acted much more like editors or even revisers than like compositors or amanuenses, and altered, abbreviated, and interpolated their texts according to their taste and fancy, in far more essential matters than spelling and grammar. (6) What corresponded to modern proof-reading was a good deal less a matter of course than it is now, and, on the whole, a good deal less painstaking. It would be harsh to

[1] A good example of this is the ME (the 'Chaucerian') translation of the *Roman de la Rose*, a translation for whose text we must depend, here and there, on William Thynne's collected edition of Chaucer's works (1532) because the sole surviving MS (Hunterian Museum, Glasgow, V. 3. 7) lacks certain passages. Thynne's print has 'ms authority' (as having been set up from a ms no longer extant), but has the authority that only *one* ms, apart from the Glasgow, would have – not the authority of as many mss as there are extant copies of Thynne. To be sure, the several extant copies of Thynne may differ, even copies of the same printing, as early printed books do much oftener than modern ones, because, the conditions of printing being what they were up to the nineteenth century (i.e., up to the invention of the stereotype), it was easy to interrupt – and printers often interrupted – a single printing (or 'run') in order to alter the text, either of their own motion (on the discovery of errors) or at the author's behest or in prudential or enforced consideration of 'the authorities'.

call this laziness or carelessness, for of course each single ms copy had to be 'proof-read' by and for itself alone, with a consequent expenditure of labour hardly practical, especially in a commercial scriptorium. (7) Authors not seldom altered their autographs after some, but only some, copies had been made, so that late copies show different readings – which in such a case are, of course, at least as authentic as the earlier ones. (8) In binding and rebinding, sheets (and quires) were sometimes misfolded or misplaced or even omitted.

How important such an omission may be, or the belief that one has occurred, is exemplified in Professor J. M. Manly's theory, set forth in the *Cambridge History of English Literature*, vol. 2 (1908), that *Piers Plowman* was the work, not of one poet but of four (not counting an unimportant fifth, whose existence everyone admits) – a theory based chiefly on Professor Manly's opinion that a leaf – or rather a sheet – was lost from the autograph of the earliest of the five poets hypothetically assumed. The theory has been attacked and rejected by many scholars, and perhaps somewhat damaged, but Professor Manly's argument is still very impressive.

Such errors in binding and rebinding were facilitated by a usual absence of pagination, a frequent absence of 'foliation' (i.e., the numbering of leaves – in other words, of every other page), the frequent absence also of 'catchwords' (i.e., the first word of a page written also at the bottom of the preceding one), the cutting away, in binding or rebinding, both of the catchwords and of the 'signature marks' (i.e., letters and numbers placed on at least the first half of each sheet to guide the binder) – etc., etc.

In the light of all these occasions of corruption and confusion, and when one considers that, even with works recorded in scores of extant mss, we seldom find two of which one was copied from the other – i.e., that most copies were made from copies, not from the original, and that most copies from either the original or any given earlier copy have disappeared – one may begin to get some faint notion of how hard it is to establish exactly what a ME or other mediaeval writer wrote. With a work extant in only one ms – a copy, not the original – the original text can usually not be established with even an approach to certainty;

with a work extant in many mss (such as *Piers Plowman* and the *Canterbury Tales*, each extant in scores of copies of a wildly various provenience) it sometimes can, but only at the expense of enormous toil. The original text of *Piers Plowman* can probably never be so; that of the *Canterbury Tales* has been, pretty well, but only by the prodigious exertions of Professors Manly and Rickert of the University of Chicago, recorded in eight volumes totalling some 4,000 pages, of which the actual text – the end result of the whole operation – occupies a pathetically small fraction, most of the space being given to almost interminable lists of variants, detailed descriptions and histories of mss, prolegomena of various kinds, etc., etc.[1]

And even a text elicited by such herculean labours may be attacked and rejected by scholars who disagree with the producer about certain fundamental principles of what the procedure should be. The first step in establishing a text from many and very different mss has to be some kind of classification of the mss: i.e., a sorting out of them according to the similarity of their texts, with special reference to their probable direct or indirect dependence on mss no longer extant. For a long time the universal method of doing this was to group the mss by identical (and manifest) errors, on the principle that two mss both giving a clearly right reading, or giving, each, a *different* clearly wrong one, are not necessarily connected with each other (except, of course, in so far as they both derive ultimately from the author's autograph) but that two mss exhibiting the *same* errors *are* probably connected in a comparatively close degree. But since about 1913 a good deal of impressive criticism has been directed against some of the applications of this principle or of principles nearly related to it, and consequently there is now a good deal more uncertainty and disagreement than there was earlier in the century as to how to go about establishing a text and how to know when you have established it.[2]

[1] J. M. Manly and Edith Rickert, *The Text of the Canterbury Tales, Studied on the Basis of All the Known Manuscripts*, Chicago, 1940.

[2] See the Rev. H. J. Chaytor, *From Script to Print*, Cambridge, 1945, pp. 148ff., for a short but illuminating summary of controversy about textual criticism and for further references. See also Manly and Rickert's *The Text of the Canterbury Tales* (cited above), vol. 2, pp. 12ff.

A few words should be added about the physical form and appearance of mediaeval books in so far as they differ conspicuously from those of modern ones. (1) The materials were parchment or vellum universally (in Europe) up to the twelfth century and usually up to the fourteenth (and often well into the fifteenth); increasingly paper thereafter. *Parchment* is properly and originally a general name for any animal hide prepared for writing, though it is, especially nowadays, sometimes – but only sometimes – restricted to the coarse and common and hence comparatively cheap skins of full-grown sheep and goats, the name *vellum* (literally calfskin) being then applied to the finer, scarcer, sometimes smaller, often more carefully prepared, and dearer skins not only of calves but also of kids and lambs. Parchment (even in the inclusive sense) was naturally very costly, as compared with modern paper; and mediaeval paper (fortunately always rag, never wood-pulp, else very few mediaeval paper mss would still exist, at any rate in good condition) was not cheap; hence mediaeval books often come down to us stripped of their fly-leaves and even, now and then, with their sometimes wide original margins missing, through the offices of owners – or borrowers! – hard up for writing materials. From the fourteenth century on, mss sometimes contain some sheets or quires of parchment and others of paper. But even paper was used by no means as prodigally as it is today; note-taking and rough drafting were often done with a stylus on thin boards coated with wax ('tablets'), which could be smoothed down and re-used indefinitely.

Mss meant for binding (as of course the usual literary ms was), like printed books, were not ordinarily first bound and then written in, as a modern ledger is, but written on the successive surfaces of the sheets of the several quires, which were later assembled: obviously, if a book is to be bound securely by any other means than some very recent ones, it must be made up of sheets *folded* at least once so that they may be firmly and neatly sewn together through the fold; and to reduce both the labour of sewing and the comparative thickness of the folded edges, four sheets (sometimes fewer or more – often many more when the material was paper) were usually folded together, one inside another, making what is called a quire or gathering (though strictly speaking, a 'quire' ought to be a gathering of only four sheets). Now if you take four sheets and fold them so, once, you will have a little booklet of four sheets, or eight leaves, or sixteen pages; and naturally, the outermost sheet will contain pp. 1, 2, 15, and 16, the next to the outermost pp. 3, 4, 13, and 14, and so on. Here is obviously danger of confusion on the part of both scribe and binder.

Books were bound by sewing the several folded sheets of each quire together through the fold and then knotting the ends of the thread around three or more cords (or strips of parchment) stretched horizontal to the back (or 'spine') of the book. Small books were usually, and large ones sometimes, covered with (often stiffened) parchment, usually a little larger than the page size, so as to provide a protective overhang at the edges, in the style of many modern Bibles; large ones in (often leather-covered) boards. (Later the term 'boards' came to apply not only to wood but also to pasteboard.) But even a book whose front and back covers were of boards necessarily had a more or less flexible outer spine of leather, which was commonly moulded so as to keep the cords from breaking through, and these raised mouldings were often gilded or otherwise decorated. Hence the horizontal lines often seen on the spines of modern book covers – though here they do not usually project, or at least need not, and are merely ornamental, because, in almost all modern books, the cords (which are now often mere threads themselves), instead of protruding, are sunk into channels sawn across the spine. Technically speaking, most modern books are not 'bound', but 'cased', the outer covering of the spine being quite free of the spine itself, whereas in most mediaeval codices the covering bends with the spine.

Mediaeval books were produced in almost as wide a range of sizes as modern ones, but the average, at least for strictly literary works – e.g., the extant mss of the *Canterbury Tales* – was about 8 inches by 11 inches, or perhaps a very little less – a good deal larger than most modern books. A page of this size has usually some thirty or thirty-five lines – a good many fewer than the average modern printed page despite the latter's being smaller, as it can be because most modern type is much smaller than most mediaeval handwriting.

The ink used in most mediaeval mss, though originally black, is now brown, because of its chemical constitution. Sometimes, when it has been erased, it can be made visible again by ultra-violet photography, or, when it is not distinguishable by the eye from blemishes in the parchment, it can be made so by infra-red. Occasionally, words obscured or lost can be ascertained by studying the 'offset', i.e., the mirror-image of writing produced by the long contact of two pages.

The typical mediaeval ms book also differs from the typical modern one in having no formal and separate title page (and often no title, properly speaking), often no author's name, no notation of place and date of publication, no table of contents,[1] and usually no index; and most of the kind of thing that we should put into footnotes was put into the margin – or parenthetically into the text (but without parentheses!), with the result that many mediaeval works, unless resourcefully and imaginatively edited and 'designed' (typographically), seem a good deal more incoherent than they actually were in conception.

It has been said that titles and authors' names were often absent. This is largely due not to any modesty on the part of mediaeval writers, but rather to (1) the frequent unconcern of mediaeval scribes as to who had written the book they were copying, and (2) the natural tendency of the first (and last) leaves of books to become separated from the rest, owing to hard use and the frequent loss or feebleness or even original absence of adequate covers – and to the occasional abstraction

---

[1] How unusual, impressive, and mysterious such a simple device as a table of contents might be is prettily exemplified by the introduction to such a table in Dan Michel's *The Ayenbite of Inwit* (1340), already mentioned. 'þise byeþ,' says Dan Michel portentously, 'þe capiteles of þe boc volȝinde. And byeþ y-wryte to vynde y-redliche by þe tellynge of algorisme ine huyche leaue of þe boc þet hy by. And in huyche half of þe lyeaue be tuaye lettres of þe abece. þet is to wytene .A. and .b. .A. betocneþ þe verste half of þe leaue .b. þe oþerhalf.' ('These are the chapters of the following book. They are set down here in order that the reader may easily find, by the use of arabic numerals, which leaf each begins on; and on which side of the leaf, by two letters of the alphabet, that is to say, *a* and *b*, *a* meaning the first side and *b* the second.')

of fly-leaves (and resultant loosening of the stitching) by parchment- or paper-starved users. Partly because of such accidents, book titles in the middle ages tend to be less stable and uniform than we normally expect them to be today, and often amounted to common-sense and hence verbally variable descriptions rather than unalterable phrases; thus the poem of Chaucer's commonly called nowadays *The Legend of Good Women* is also called, both in some mss and by Chaucer himself, 'the seyntes legend of Cupide' (i.e., the legend of Cupid's saints). And sometimes even such descriptions were thought insufficient, so that a book might be alternatively or additionally identified, in a reference by another writer, by its opening and closing phrases – e.g., the book by the late-twelfth-century Andreas Capellanus commonly called *De arte honeste amandi* ('how well-bred people should conduct their love affairs') is cited by a late-thirteenth-century critic as 'Librum De amore sive de Deo amoris qui sic incipit: *Cogit me multum*, etc., et sic terminatur: *Cave igitur, Gualteri, amoris exercere mandata*'.[1]

When titles and authors' names are found, they are (1) found often at the end as well as or even sometimes instead of at the beginning, and (2) are usually not independent phrases but contained in sentences starting with *Hic incipit* or *Here beginneth* such and such a book by such and such a writer, and *Hic explicit* or *Here endeth*, etc.; and each of the chapters or other divisions often begins and ends with similar formulae.[2] These formulae, as implied above, are often in Latin even when the text is in

---

[1] Quoted from J. J. Parry, *The Art of Courtly Love by Andreas Capellanus*, N.Y., 1941, pp. 21–22.

[2] One further observation about these *hic* and *here* formulae is that their frequency in mss is very possibly owing at least indirectly to their natural and common enunciation by a public reader (cf. the familiar rubrics in the Book of Common Prayer) for whose use many mss were primarily intended. Much the same circumstances probably account for the frequency with which mediaeval narratives (e.g., almost all Chaucer's Canterbury Tales) conclude with some sort of benediction pronounced by the teller on his readers – originally on his company of hearers. This benediction is usually religious in tone if not in diction, and perhaps owes something to the common mediaeval practice of using stories, sometimes of a decidedly worldly tenor, as illustrative *exempla* in popular sermons.

English or some other vernacular: a vestige of this rather point-less and snobbish practice remains in modern printed books in the occasional use of the Latin *finis* at the bottom of the last page. It is somewhat as if mediaeval scribes (followed, in the case of *finis*, by some modern printers) were saying, 'Latin, of course, is the only language really worth copying.'

To be sure, luckily for the history of English literature, the scribes didn't really think so.

READING LIST

THE FOLLOWING list is by design highly selective, and to some extent arbitrary. It includes, for the most part, two kinds of books: (1) Those particularly practical for the elementary or amateur student (these are distinguished by an asterisk), and (2) more or less advanced but fundamental works of scholarship that the elementary or amateur student should at least know to exist. Books in other languages than English have for the most part been deliberately excluded.

OE AND ME BIBLIOGRAPHY

*W. L. Renwick and Harold Orton. *The Beginnings of English Literature to Skelton*, 1509. Rev. ed., London, 1952. (Vol. 1 of *Introductions to English Literature*, ed. Bonamy Dobrée.) (Infinite riches in a little room; the single most valuable and convenient aid and guide to the study of Early English generally, both language and literature.)

Cambridge Bibliography of English Literature, vol. 1, London, 1941; vol. 5 (supplement to 1954), London, 1957.

OE BIBLIOGRAPHY

A. H. Heusinkveld and E. J. Bashe. *A Bibliographical Guide to Old English: A Selective Bibliography of the Language, Literature, and History of the Anglo-Saxons*. Iowa City, 1931.

ME BIBLIOGRAPHY

* J. E. Wells. *A Manual of the Writings in Middle English*, 1050–1400. New Haven, 1916. Also nine *Supplements*, New Haven, 1916–52, covering scholarly production through 1945. (Contains, besides exhaustive bibliography, helpful descriptions and abstracts of practically every extant piece of ME literature.)

THE HISTORICAL STUDY OF LANGUAGE GENERALLY

H. C. Wyld. *The Historical Study of the Mother Tongue: An Introduction to Philological Method*. London, 1906. (Though this deals chiefly and immediately with English, it affords a matchless introduction to and justification of the methods of historical linguistics generally.)

Edward Sapir. *Language*. New York, 1921.
Leonard Bloomfield. *Language*. London, 1933.
L. H. Gray. *Foundations of Language*. New York, 1939.
J. P. Hughes. *The Science of Language*. New York, 1962.
R. H. Robins. *General Linguistics*. London, 1964.

PHONETICS

* Daniel Jones. *The Pronunciation of English*. Cambridge, 1950.
(An excellent introduction to phonetics generally as well as to
that of NE specifically.)

IE PHILOLOGY

Antoine Meillet. *Introduction à l'étude comparative des langues
indo-européennes*. 8th ed., Paris, 1937. (There is no strictly
comparable work in English.)

GERMANIC PHILOLOGY

Eduard Prokosch. *A Comparative Germanic Grammar*. Phila-
delphia, 1939. (Contains also much additional information
about IE.)

GENERAL HISTORY OF ENGLISH

(The first seven books below are general histories of the English
language, and deal with NE at a good deal greater length than
with OE or ME. They are arranged in the order of increasing
length and elaborateness.)

* Ernest Weekley. *The English Language*. Rev. ed., with a
chapter on the history of American English by John W. Clark.
London, 1952. (In *The Language Library*, ed. Eric Partridge,
André Deutsch Ltd.)

* Henry Bradley. *The Making of English*. London, 1904. (A
little old, but a classic.)

* Otto Jespersen. *Growth and Structure of the English Language*.
Ninth ed., London, 1938. (Another classic, somewhat more
recent.)

* Simeon Potter. *Our Language*. Penguin Books (Pelican),
Harmondsworth, Middlesex, 1950.

* G. L. Brook. *A History of the English Language*. London, 1958.
(In *The Language Library*, ed. Eric Partridge, André Deutsch
Ltd.)

Stuart Robertson. *The Development of Modern English*. Second ed., revised by F. G. Cassidy, New York, 1954.

A. C. Baugh. *A History of the English Language*. Second ed., New York and London, 1957.

H. C. Wyld. *A Short History of English*. Third ed., London, 1927. (Almost uniquely informative and suggestive about sounds and forms, but contains scarcely anything about vocabulary and syntax, and is hardly for the elementary student.)

Samuel Moore, rev. ed., A. H. Marckwardt. *Historical Outline of English Sounds and Inflections*. Ann Arbor, 1951. (Earlier edd. have the titles *Historical Outlines of English Phonology and Middle English Grammar* and *Historical Outlines of English Phonology and Morphology*. Somewhat like the immediately preceding book in scope, but rather more elementary and tabular and less speculative.)

THE ENGLISH VOCABULARY

* M. S. Serjeantson. *A History of Foreign Words in English*. London, 1935. (Reprinted New York, 1961.)

* J. B. Greenough and G. L. Kittredge. *Words and Their Ways in English Speech*. Boston and London, 1902. (Deals chiefly with NE, but a very readable book, and by way of being a classic.)

J. A. Sheard. *The Words We Use*. London, 1954. (In *The Language Library*, ed. Eric Partridge: André Deutsch Ltd.)

T. H. Savory. *The Language of Science*. London. Revised edition, 1966. (In *The Language Library*, ed. Eric Partridge; André Deutsch Ltd. Deals with the development of the scientific vocabulary of English from OE through NE.)

OE GRAMMAR

Joseph and Elizabeth Mary Wright. *Old English Grammar*. Third ed., Oxford, 1925. (Standard but advanced.)

Randolph Quirk and C. L. Wrenn. *An Old English Grammar*. Second ed., London, 1958. (Recent and concise.)

Alistair Campbell. *Old English Grammar*. Oxford, 1959. (Recent and exhaustive.)

* Samuel Moore and T. A. Knott. *The Elements of Old English.* Ninth ed., Ann Arbor, 1942. (Includes 'Elementary Grammar' on the French-without-tears principle, 'Reference Grammar' (a sort of abstract of Wright), select passages of OE prose and verse, and glossary.)

OE DICTIONARIES

(There is no altogether satisfactory OE dictionary; each of the books listed below has different merits, as indicated.)

T. N. Toller. *An Anglo-Saxon Dictionary Based on the Manuscript Collections of the Late Joseph Bosworth.* Oxford, 1882–98, with *Supplements*, Oxford, 1908–20. (Standard; fullest. Commonly cited as 'Bosworth-Toller'.)

* J. R. Clark Hall. *A Concise Anglo-Saxon Dictionary for the Use of Students.* Fourth ed., Cambridge, 1960. (Best for all but advanced students.)

C. W. M. Grein. *Sprachschatz der Angelsächsischen Dichter.* New ed., J. J. Köhler and Ferdinand Holthausen, Heidelberg, 1912. (Complete for OE verse. Most of the definitions are in Latin rather than in either German or English.)

Ferdinand Holthausen. *Altenglisches Etymologisches Wörterbuch.* Heidelberg, 1934. (A marvel of excellence within its comparatively narrow scope, but of little practical use to the beginner even if he reads German, since few compounds are included).

OE ANTHOLOGIES

* W. J. Sedgefield. *An Anglo-Saxon Book of Verse and Prose.* Manchester, 1928.

A. J. Wyatt. *An Anglo-Saxon Reader.* Cambridge, 1925.

Henry Sweet. *An Anglo-Saxon Reader.* Fifteenth ed., revised by Dorothy Whitelock, Oxford, 1967.

W. F. Bolton. *An Old English Anthology.* London, 1963.

OTHER OE TEXTS

G. P. Krapp and E. van K. Dobbie. *The Anglo-Saxon Poetic Records.* Six volumes, Columbia University Press, New York, 1931–54. (The only recent complete collection of OE verse; contains the standard text of many poems. Introductions and notes, but no glossary.)

Friedrich Klaeber. *Beowulf and the Fight at Finnsburg*. Third ed., New York and London, 1936 (and with supplements, 1941 and 1950). (The most elaborate edition.)

NE RENDERINGS OF OE VERSE

George Sampson. *The Cambridge Book of Prose and Verse*. (See ME ANTHOLOGIES below.)

* R. K. Gordon. *Anglo-Saxon Poetry*. London, 1927. (*Everyman's Library*, no. 794.) (Prose rendering of most OE verse.)

* C. W. Kennedy. *An Anthology of Old English Poetry*. New York, 1960. (In alliterative verse.)

* C. W. Kennedy. *Beowulf . . . Translated into Alliterative Verse with a Critical Introduction*. New York. 1940.

* J. R. Clark Hall. *Beowulf . . . A Translation into Modern English Prose*. New ed., rev. C. L. Wrenn, with preface by J. R. R. Tolkien, London, 1940.

David Wright. *Beowulf: A Prose Translation with an Introduction*. Penguin Books, 1957.

OE LITERATURE: HISTORY AND CRITICISM

* W. L. Renwick and Harold Orton. *The Beginnings of English Literature to Skelton*, 1509. (See OE AND ME BIBLIOGRAPHY above.)

G. K. Anderson. *The Literature of the Anglo-Saxons*. Princeton and Oxford University Presses, 1949.

W. P. Ker. *English Literature, Medieval*. (See ME LITERATURE: HISTORY AND CRITICISM below.)

* S. A. Brooke. *English Literature from the Beginning to the Norman Conquest*. London, 1898. (Old but good.)

Bernhard Ten Brink. *Early English Literature*. Tr. H. M. Kennedy. London, 1883. (Even older than Brooke, but a classic.)

C. W. Kennedy. *The Earliest English Poetry: a Critical Survey of the Poetry Written before the Norman Conquest with Illustrative Translations*. Oxford University Press, 1943.

Cambridge History of English Literature, vol. 1. Cambridge, 1907.

* Kemp Malone. 'The Old English Period (to 1100)', in A. C. Baugh, ed., *A Literary History of England*, New York and London, 1948.

S. B. Greenfield. *A Critical History of Old English Literature*. New York, 1965.

ME GRAMMAR

Fernand Mossé. *A Handbook of Middle English.* Tr. J. A. Walker. The Johns Hopkins Press, Baltimore, 1952.

* E. E. Wardale. *An Introduction to Middle English Grammar.* London, 1937.

Joseph and Elizabeth Mary Wright. *An Elementary Middle English Grammar.* Second ed., Oxford, 1928.

Samuel Moore, S. B. Meech, and Harold Whitehall. *Middle English Dialect Characteristics and Dialect Boundaries.* University of Michigan Press, Ann Arbor, 1935. (The gist of this is more conveniently accessible in Mossé, above, and in Moore (rev. Marckwardt) (see GENERAL HISTORY OF ENGLISH above), as well as in *Middle English Dictionary* (see ME DICTIONARIES below).)

O. F. Emerson. *A Middle English Reader.* (See ME ANTHOLOGIES below.)

Kenneth Sisam. *Fourteenth Century Verse and Prose.* (See ME ANTHOLOGIES below.)

Bruce Dickins and R. M. Wilson. *Early Middle English Texts.* (See ME ANTHOLOGIES below.)

ME DICTIONARIES

(One must depend chiefly on the glossaries of the several texts; the best ME dictionary is still the ME entries in the *Oxford English Dictionary* (formerly *A New English Dictionary*), thirteen volumes including supplement, Oxford, 1933. *Middle English Dictionary*, University of Michigan Press, Ann Arbor, 1952– will eventually take its place (for ME), but not, at the present rate of publication, much before 1990: in the spring of 1966, only A–G and a part of H of the dictionary proper had been published, though the 'Plan and Bibliography' appeared in 1954; it contains a handy abstract, with maps, of the work of Samuel Moore, *et al.*, on ME dialects, as noted under ME GRAMMAR above.)

MEDIAEVAL LITERATURE GENERALLY

E. R. Curtius. *European Literature and the Latin Middle Ages.* Tr. W. R. Trask. New York, 1958. (Bollingen Series XXXVI, Pantheon Press.) (A work of stupendous scope and erudition.

The sections on OE and ME literature are slight, but serve to connect them with ancient and mediaeval European literature generally.)

H. J. Chaytor. *From Script to Print: An Introduction to Medieval Vernacular Literature.* Cambridge, 1945. ('... an attempt to show the importance of the difference between the literary and critical methods of the early middle ages and those of modern times. Any such attempt must necessarily make French literature the point of departure.' Ignorance of Old French will prevent the beginner's profiting from much of this book, but by no means all of it.)

ME ANTHOLOGIES

Fernand Mossé. *A Handbook of Middle English.* (See ME GRAMMAR above.)

O. F. Emerson. *A Middle English Reader . . . with Grammatical Introduction, Notes, and Glossary.* Rev. ed., New York, 1915. (Contains also detailed account of ME grammar.)

Alois Brandl and Otto Zippel. *Mittelenglische Sprach- und Literaturproben.* Second ed., Berlin, 1927. Reprinted as *Middle English Literature*, Chelsea Publishing Co., New York, 1947. (Despite the German title, everything, including introductions and glossary – which is also the best etymological glossary to Chaucer – is in English except the Preface. No explanatory notes, but adequate introductions and many parallel passages from French and Latin sources. The most comprehensive and respresentative and in some ways illuminating collection, but not in all ways suitable for the beginner.)

* A. S. Cook. *A Literary Middle English Reader.* Boston, 1915 (reprinted 1943). (Difficult words glossed at the foot of the page; an entertaining book.)

* George Sampson. *The Cambridge Book of Prose and Verse, in Illustration of English Literature from the Beginnings to the Cycles of Romance.* Cambridge, 1924. (Designed to illustrate the *Cambridge History of English Literature*, volumes 1 and 2. Difficult words glossed at the foot of the page. Contains also NE renderings of a considerable number of OE writings.)

Joseph Hall. *Selections from Early Middle English.* Two volumes, Oxford, 1920. (A work of great learning, likely to remain standard for many years, but not for the beginner. Abundant notes, but no glosses or glossary.)

* Bruce Dickins and R. M. Wilson. *Early Middle English Texts.* Second ed., Cambridge, 1959. (Much easier going than Hall; with Sisam (see below), probably the most practical ME textbook beyond the elementary level and short of the professional. Contains also summary of 'Characteristics of Early Middle English'.)

* Kenneth Sisam. *Fourteenth Century Verse and Prose.* Oxford, 1921; with vocabulary by J. R. R. Tolkien, Oxford, 1922. (See Dickins and Wilson above. Also contains short but clear sketch of fourteenth-century English grammar.)

Boris Ford, ed. *The Age of Chaucer.* (*A Guide to English Literature*, vol. 1.) Penguin Books, Harmondsworth, Middlesex, 1954.

* W. H. French and C. B. Hale. *Middle English Metrical Romances.* New York, 1930.

R. W. Chambers and Marjorie Daunt. *A Book of London English*, 1384–1425. Oxford, 1931. (Mostly non-literary documents. Fascinating linguistically and sociologically.)

* Sir Edmund K. Chambers and F. Sidgwick. *Early English Lyrics.* London, 1907.

* Robert D. Stevick. *One Hundred Middle English Lyrics.* Indianapolis and New York, 1964.

W. A. Neilson and K. G. T. Webster. *Chief British Poets of the Fourteenth and Fifteenth Centuries.* Boston, 1916. (ME texts with footnote glosses, except for *Pearl, Sir Gawain and the Green Knight*, and a part of *Piers Plowman*, which are printed in NE translation.)

RENDERINGS OF ME VERSE: ANTHOLOGIES

* J. L. Weston. *The Chief Middle English Poets. Selected Poems Newly Rendered and Edited.* . . . Boston, 1914.

* J. L. Weston. *Romance, Vision and Satire. English Alliterative Poems of the Fourteenth Century.* Boston, 1912.

CHAUCER: EDITIONS

W. W. Skeat, ed. *The Complete Works of Geoffrey Chaucer.* Seven volumes (including one of the 'Chaucer apocrypha'), Oxford,

1894–97. (Commonly cited as the 'Oxford Chaucer'. The largest and in some ways still the best and standard edition.)

W. W. Skeat, ed. *The Student's Chaucer*. Oxford, 1895. (One volume. Text substantially the same as that of the Oxford Chaucer, but contains no background annotation.)

A. W. Pollard, *et al.*, edd. *The Works of Geoffrey Chaucer*. London, 1898. (Commonly cited as the 'Globe Chaucer'. In general a sounder text than Skeat's, but never in such wide use. Very little background annotation.)

* F. N. Robinson. *The Complete Works of Geoffrey Chaucer*. Second ed., Boston and Oxford, 1957. (The latest and in most ways the best and standard. Magnificently annotated.)

CHAUCER: NE RENDERINGS

(NE renderings of Chaucer ought not to be necessary, and many of them are bad. The two best ones are the following.)

* Nevill Coghill. *The Canterbury Tales, translated into Modern English*. Penguin Books, Harmondsworth, Middlesex, 1954.

* Theodore Morrison. *The Portable Chaucer*. The Viking Press, New York, 1949.

CHAUCER: CRITICISM

(A surprisingly – and gratifyingly – large number of critical books about Chaucer have been published since 1915, and particularly since 1945. Many of them, however, are not very distinguished, and others are of little interest or use to beginners. Some of the best are the following.)

* G. L. Kittredge. *Chaucer and His Poetry*. Cambridge (U.S.A.), 1915. (In some ways out of date, or at least out of fashion, but a classic.)

* J. L. Lowes. *Geoffrey Chaucer and the Development of His Genius*. Cambridge (U.S.A.), 1934.

* Nevill Coghill. *The Poet Chaucer*. (*The Home University Library*.) London, 1949.

* Derek D. Brewer. *Chaucer*. Second ed., London, 1958.

* E. T. Donaldson. *Chaucer's Poetry: An Anthology for the Modern Reader*. New York, 1958. (Listed here instead of under *Chaucer:* EDITIONS above (1) because it has a normalized text and, as its title indicates, an incomplete one and (2) because its peculiar importance and excellence lie in 'Part II: Commentary,' pp. 841–980, especially pp. 871–980.)

PIERS PLOWMAN

W. W. Skeat, ed. *The Vision of William concerning Piers the Plowman.* Two volumes, Oxford, 1896. (New texts are badly needed, and have been so for many years; two newly edited 'A' texts have appeared (1952 and 1960), but for 'B' and 'C' texts one must still depend mainly, and for a handy conspectus of the three entirely, on Skeat.)

Donald and Rachel Attwater. *The Book concerning Piers the Plowman.* Everyman's Library, London and New York, 1957. (NE rendering of the 'B' text in alliterative verse.)

* J. F. Goodridge. *Piers the Ploughman . . . Translated into Modern English with an Introduction.* Penguin Books, 1957. (Prose; 'B' text; full and admirable introduction and other apparatus.)

PEARL and SIR GAWAIN AND THE GREEN KNIGHT

E. V. Gordon, ed. *Pearl.* Oxford, 1954.

Sir Israel Gollancz, ed. *Pearl . . . with Modern English Rendering. . . .* Rev. ed., London, 1921.

J. R. R. Tolkien and E. V. Gordon, edd. *Sir Gawain and the Green Knight.* Corrected ed., Oxford, 1930.

T. H. Banks, Jr. *Sir Gawain and the Green Knight.* New York, 1929. (NE verse rendering.)

J. L. Rosenberg. *Sir Gawain and the Green Knight.* New York and Toronto, 1959. (NE verse rendering, with introduction by J. R. Kreuzer.)

* A. C. Cawley, ed. *Pearl* [and] *Sir Gawain and the Green Knight.* Everyman's Library, London and New York, 1962. (Text accompanied by marginal glosses and copious and useful footnote paraphrases; an excellent compromise (particularly in *Pearl*), for the beginner, between text alone and NE rendering alone, especially one in verse.)

ME LITERATURE GENERALLY: HISTORY AND CRITICISM

* W. L. Renwick and Harold Orton. *The Beginnings of English Literature to Skelton,* 1509. (See OE AND ME BIBLIOGRAPHY above.)

* W. P. Ker. *English Literature, Medieval.* (*The Home University Library.*) London, 1904; reset, with a supplementary note by

R. W. Chambers, London, 1945. (Old and short, but deservedly accounted a classic.)

* W. H. Schofield. *English Literature from the Norman Conquest to Chaucer*. New York and London, 1906. (Old, but not yet supplanted by anything quite like it in scope and scale. Contains much on Anglo-Norman and Anglo-Latin literature as well as on ME.)

Bernhard Ten Brink. *Early English Literature*. (See OE LITERATURE: HISTORY AND CRITICISM above.)

Cambridge History of English Literature. Vol. 1, Cambridge, 1907; vol. 2, Cambridge, 1908.

* A. C. Baugh. 'The Middle English Period', in A. C. Baugh, ed., *A Literary History of England*, New York and London, 1948

Carleton Brown and R. H. Robbins. *The Index of Middle English Verse*. New York, 1943.

R. M. Wilson. *Early Middle English Literature*. Second ed., London, 1951.

H. S. Bennett. *Chaucer and the Fifteenth Century*. (*Oxford History of English Literature*, vol. 2, part 1.) Oxford, 1947.

Boris Ford, ed. *The Age of Chaucer*. (See ME ANTHOLOGIES above.)

W. W. Lawrence. *Mediaeval Story*. Rev. ed., New York, 1926.

* A. B. Taylor. *An Introduction to Medieval Romance*. London, 1930.

George Kane. *Middle English Literature: A Critical Study of the Romances, the Religious Lyrics, Piers Plowman*. London, 1951.

J. P. Oakden. *Alliterative Poetry in Middle English: The Dialectal and Metrical Survey*. Manchester University Press, 1930. (Neither this nor, in less measure, the following book is for the beginner.)

J. P. Oakden, with the assistance of E. R. Innes. *Alliterative Poetry in Middle English: A Survey of the Traditions*. Manchester University Press, 1935.

G. P. Krapp. *The Rise of English Literary Prose*. Oxford, 1916. (The thesis is practically that NE literary prose sprang from Wyclif.)

R. W. Chambers. *On the Continuity of English Prose.* London, 1932. (Controverts Krapp; finds the springs of NE literary prose in LOE and EME homily.)

J. W. H. Atkins. *English Literary Criticism: The Mediaeval Phase.* Cambridge, 1942. (On Latin literature, not on English; a fact in itself of great significance.)

This index does not include words used as illustrative examples and it contains no references to the Reading List.

S. Potter
21.xi.66